Contents

Features.. 2
Standards.. 4

Unit One: Take a Stand 6
Something Rotten at Village Market
Comparing and Contrasting..................... 8
Vocabulary Builder.................................. 9
"Starting with a Bang"........................... 10
Thinking About the Selection................. 15
Writing an Informational Essay.............. 16
Strategy Workout: Character 18
Homonyms... 19

A Teen's Guide to Working
Comparing and Contrasting................... 20
Vocabulary Builder................................ 21
"Why Work?"... 22
Thinking About the Selection................. 27
Writing a Business Letter 28
Strategy Workout: Research Skills
   and Strategies 30
Synonyms and Antonyms 31

Space Play
Identifying Cause and Effect.................. 32
Vocabulary Builder................................ 33
"In the Virtual-Reality Room" 34
Thinking About the Selection................. 39
Writing Instructions............................... 40
Strategy Workout: Setting...................... 42
Figurative Language.............................. 43

The Moon and Beyond
Identifying Cause and Effect.................. 44
Vocabulary Builder................................ 45
"The Race to Space"............................... 46
Thinking About the Selection..................51
Writing a Summary................................ 52
Strategy Workout: Pictures, Charts,
   and Graphs 54
Using Context Clues 55

Take a Stand—Wrap-Up
"What a Difference a Year Makes" 56
"Lend a Hand".......................................61

Unit Two:
Why Me?
Making Inferences, Drawing Conclusions........... 68
Vocabulary Builder................................ 69
"The Visit"... 70
Thinking About the Selection................. 75
Writing a Speech 76
Strategy Workout: Plot 78
Compound Words 79

And Justice for All
Making Inferences, Drawing Conclusions........... 80
Vocabulary Builder.................................81
"The Crime Scene and Evidence"........... 82
Thinking About the Selection................. 87
Writing a Persuasive Essay 88
Strategy Workout: Headers 90
Reference Materials: Encyclopedias.......91

Tales from Gull Island
Recognizing Author's Viewpoint, Purpose 92
Vocabulary Builder................................ 93
"How Coyote Learned the River Code" 94
Thinking About the Selection................. 99
Writing a Review.................................. 100
Strategy Workout: Theme 102
Understanding Words with More Than
   One Meaning 103

From Zeus to Aliens
Recognizing Author's Viewpoint, Purpose 104
Vocabulary Builder...............................105
"Old Myths and Modern Monsters" 106
Thinking About the Selection............... 111
Writing a Myth 112
Strategy Workout: Table of Contents
   and Index 114
Prefixes and Suffixes 115

Respect All Voices—Wrap-Up
"What Does the Truth Have to Do with It?"...... 116
"Animal Rights, Animals Wronged"....121

Answer Key... 126

Features

The *Steck-Vaughn Reading Workout* series includes four books that have been carefully leveled to ensure readability and increase the likelihood of success. The series is designed to reach middle-school students who need practice with reading strategies and other literacy skills. The passages are high-interest/low readability to promote interest. The reading levels for each book are as follows:

Book	Grade Level
1	2.5–3.0
2	3.0–3.5
3	3.5–4.5
4	4.5–5.5

Steck-Vaughn Reading Workout is organized into two units with two fiction and two nonfiction selections per theme. Each selection is supported by the following activity pages.

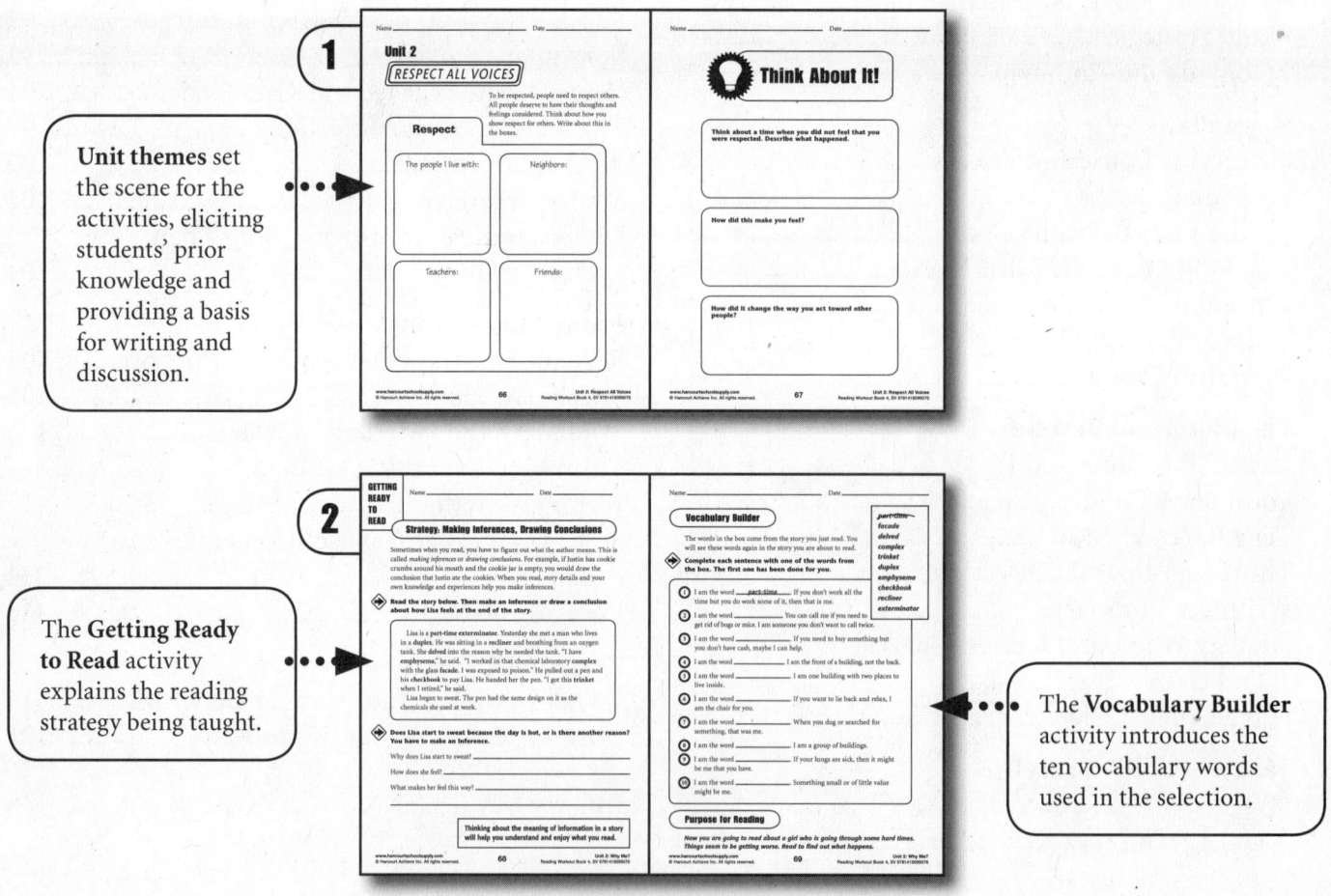

Unit themes set the scene for the activities, eliciting students' prior knowledge and providing a basis for writing and discussion.

The **Getting Ready to Read** activity explains the reading strategy being taught.

The **Vocabulary Builder** activity introduces the ten vocabulary words used in the selection.

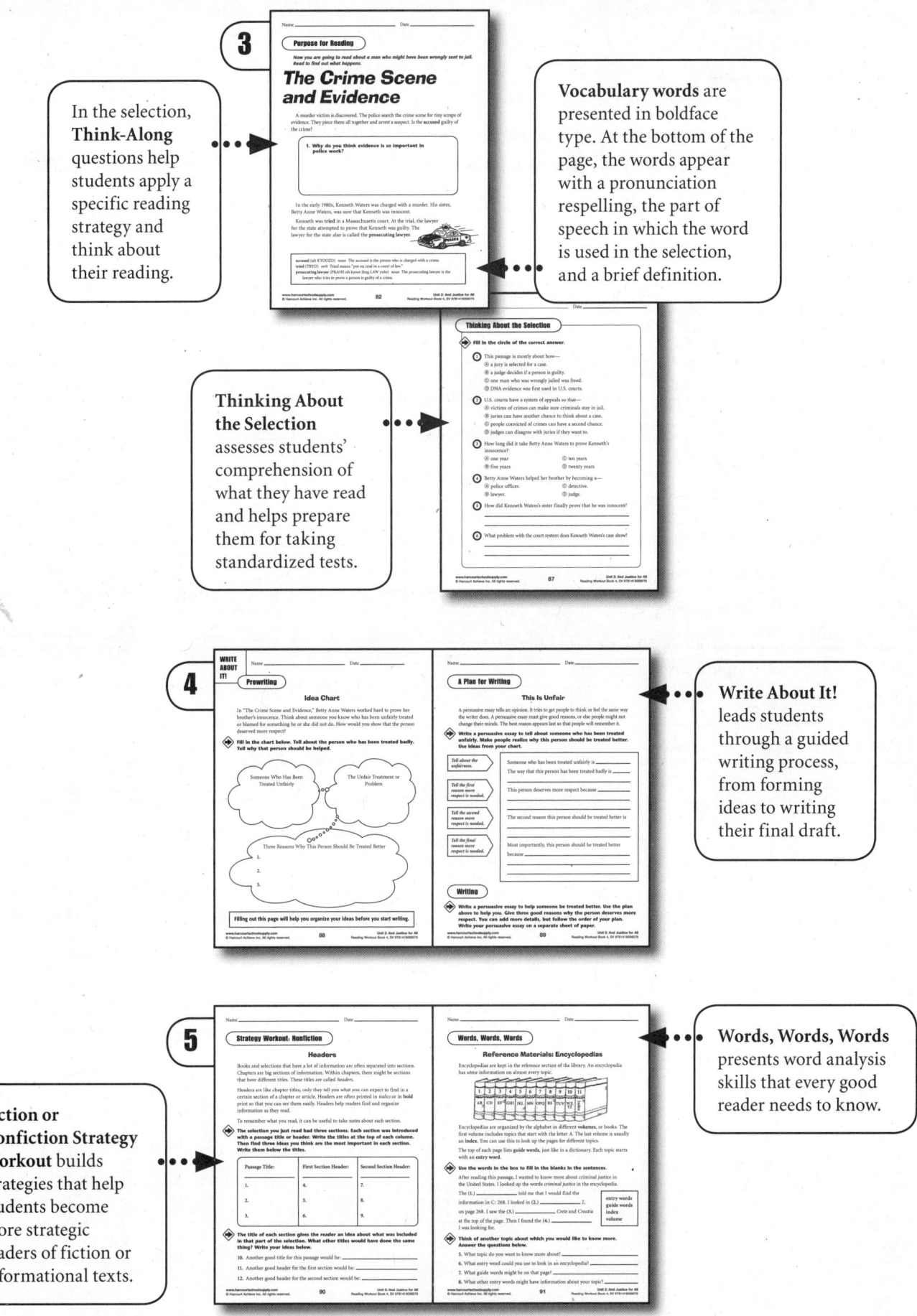

Standards

Strategy/Skill	Book 1	Book 2	Book 3	Book 4
GENERAL READING STRATEGIES				
Making predictions	X		X	
Recognizing sequence	X		X	
Identifying main idea and details	X		X	
Identifying facts and opinions	X		X	
Comparing and contrasting		X		X
Identifying cause and effect		X		X
Making inferences/drawing conclusions		X		X
Recognizing author's viewpoint and purpose		X		X
READING STRATEGIES: NONFICTION				
Using headers and subheaders to guide reading			X	X
Using informational text features (including table of contents, index, and glossary)			X	X
Interpreting pictures, graphs, and charts			X	X
Using research skills and strategies to extend a topic			X	X
READING STRATEGIES: FICTION				
Story plot			X	X
Setting			X	X
Character			X	X
Theme			X	X
WRITING FORMS				
Informational Essays	X	X	X	X
Narratives (stories, real or imagined)	X	X	X	X
Letters	X	X	X	X
Summaries	X	X	X	X
Instructions	X	X	X	X
Reviews	X	X	X	X
Persuasive Essays	X	X	X	X
Speeches	X	X	X	X

Strategy/Skill	Book 1	Book 2	Book 3	Book 4
WORD IDENTIFICATION STRATEGIES: PHONICS				
Short and long *a*	X			
Short and long *e*	X			
Short and long *i*	X			
Short and long *o*	X			
Short and long *u*	X			
Variant consonants – *g*	X			
Variant consonants – *c*	X			
Variant consonants – *s*	X			
Initial, medial, and final consonant digraphs – *ph, gh*		X		
R-controlled vowels – *er, ir, ur*		X		
R-controlled vowels – *ar, or*		X		
Vowel digraph – *oo*		X		
Sounds of *ow*		X		
Sounds of *ou*		X		
Diphthongs – *oi, oy*		X		
Silent consonants – *kn, wr, gh*		X		
WORD ANALYSIS				
Using context clues	X	X	X	X
Understanding compound words	X	X	X	X
Interpreting multiple-meaning words	X	X	X	X
Identifying synonyms and antonyms	X	X	X	X
Understanding/using homonyms, homographs, and homophones	X	X	X	X
Using prefixes, suffixes, and roots of words	X	X	X	X
Interpreting figurative language (including similes and metaphors)	X	X	X	X
Using reference materials (including dictionary and thesaurus)	X	X	X	X

Name _____ Date _____

Unit 1

TAKE A STAND

Taking a stand means being a leader. It means doing what is best, even when the best is tough to do. Think about how you would take a stand in each of the situations below. Write your ideas in the boxes.

I'll Take My Stand

- When your friends want to go to a party where there might be trouble:

- When you have chores to do, but your friends don't have to do chores:

- When you were talking in class, but your friend got in trouble for it:

- When someone you work with always takes credit for your ideas:

Name _____ Date _____

Think About It!

Think about a time when you were a leader. Write how you did what was best.

How did you feel?

How did this change you?

GETTING READY TO READ

Name _____ Date _____

Strategy: Comparing and Contrasting

Thinking about how things are the same and how they are different is called *comparing* and *contrasting*. Comparing means "thinking about how things are the same." Contrasting means "thinking about how they are different."

 As you read the story below, think about it. How will the writer's new job be different from the job he has now?

> I work bagging groceries. It's not fun, but it pays well. Soon, though, I will be a **cashier**. Yesterday I **inadvertently** overheard a customer talking to another **employee** who is a cashier. The **brawny** man told her that he had climbed a **pyramid**.
>
> Later, I **hesitantly** approached the cashier at the **cash register**. I asked if many customers tell stories. "All the time," she said. "Yesterday someone told me he survived an **avalanche** caused by a mine **explosion**." How exciting! I was full of **anticipation** of my first customer. Soon I might hear such stories, too.

 Contrast the writer's job now with the job that he will have soon. On the left side, write what the writer's job is now. Then write a few words describing this job. On the right side, write what the writer's new job will be. Then describe that job. Tell how the writer thinks these jobs will be different.

1. The writer's job now is: _____

2. This job is: _____

3. The writer's new job will be: _____

4. This job will be: _____

5. How are these jobs different? _____
_____

Comparing and contrasting will help you think about what you read.

Name _____ Date _____

Vocabulary Builder

| ~~inadvertently~~ |
| pyramid |
| avalanche |
| hesitantly |
| employee |
| brawny |
| cashier |
| cash register |
| anticipation |
| explosion |

The words in the box come from the story you just read. You will see these words again in the story you are about to read.

 Write the correct word in each sentence. This will help you learn the words before you begin reading. The first one has been done for you.

1. He __inadvertently__ tipped the display over because he was not paying attention.

2. In science class I used the wrong chemical, and it caused an _____ that made a loud sound.

3. A large amount of snow and ice sliding down a hill is an _____.

4. A person who works in a store is called a store _____.

5. The boxes were stacked so there were more on the bottom, in the shape of a _____.

6. I took my comic book to the _____, who took my money and gave me change.

7. He had been working out, so he was happy when someone said he looked _____.

8. She spoke _____ because she was not sure what to say.

9. The students were full of _____ as the end of the school year neared.

10. When I asked her for change for a dollar, she opened the _____ and gave me four quarters.

Purpose for Reading

Now you are going to read about a boy who gets a new job at a market. His first day at work starts with a bang. Read to find out what happens.

Starting with a Bang

CRASH! Tony Tavarez **inadvertently** hit a can with his elbow. The can fell, and the neatly stacked **pyramid** of Smith's Tomato Sauce became a noisy mass of falling cans. Some cans wound up in the shopping carts of customers. Others tumbled into the freezer bin. Most hit the floor and rolled down the aisles of Village Market.

The **avalanche** of cans forced Tony to take a clumsy step back. He tripped and—*bang!*—he was on the floor.

"OK, kid?" a friendly voice asked. Tony glanced up and saw Benny Walsh, his boss.

"Yes, uh . . . I'm just a little embarrassed," Tony said **hesitantly**. "Plus I just lost my summer job on the first day."

"No way, Tony," Benny said. "Accidents happen." As he spoke, Benny yanked Tony up in one swift, strong action. "Let's scoop up these cans. We don't want customers falling," he said.

As Tony started stacking cans, Benny called another young **employee**. "Joe, give us some help. We had an accident."

Tony couldn't believe it. Benny had said *we* instead of blaming him!

"Thanks, Benny," he said.

"No problem," Benny chuckled. "We younger guys stick together."

---

inadvertently (ihn ad VURT nt lee) *adverb* Inadvertently means "accidentally or without meaning to."
pyramid (PIHR uh mihd) *noun* A pyramid is a structure with a square base and four triangle-shaped sides that meet at a point at the top.
avalanche (AV uh lanch) *noun* An avalanche is a large amount of something that comes down suddenly.
hesitantly (HEHZ ih tuhnt lee) *adverb* Hesitantly means "reluctantly or in a hesitating or uncertain way."
employee (ehm PLOY ee) *noun* An employee is someone who works for someone else.

Tony had just turned 14, and this was his first job. Benny was 18. He was big and **brawny**, drove a car, and had girlfriends. Tony hadn't even shaved for the first time.

> **1. Do you think Tony looks up to Benny? Tell why you think he does or does not.**

Tony had met Benny yesterday when Mr. Salinas, the owner of Village Market, showed Tony the store.

Tony had met Mrs. Brown first.

"I'm busy opening another Village Market on Fourth Street," Mr. Salinas had explained. "When I'm not here, Sylvia Brown is in charge. She's the head **cashier**."

"Tony, if you work hard, I'll let you run a **cash register** when you're 16," Mrs. Brown said as she shook hands with Tony.

Then Mr. Salinas said, "This is Benny Walsh. He's in charge of stocking shelves, bagging groceries, and keeping the store clean. Usually Benny will tell you what to do."

brawny (BRAWN ee) *adjective* A person who is brawny has large, strong muscles.
cashier (ka SHIHR) *noun* A cashier is the person you pay when you want to buy something in a store.
cash register (KASH REHJ ihs tuhr) *noun* A cash register is a machine that businesses use to keep track of and hold money made from sales.

Benny winked and said, "Tony, if you work hard, I'll make sure you never have to touch a cash register."

2. Do you think Tony will like working with Benny or with Mrs. Brown better? Tell why you think so.

Everybody laughed. Mr. Salinas gave Tony a green Village Market cap and apron. Tony was full of **anticipation**. This was his first job ever. Could he do it?

anticipation (an tihs uh PAY shuhn) *noun* Anticipation is the act of expecting or looking forward to something.

That was yesterday. Today, just hours after knocking over the cans, Tony felt good. The can **explosion** was embarrassing at first. Thanks to Benny, it didn't bother him now. Since then, he had bagged groceries, collected carts from outside the store, and helped customers load their cars.

At noon, Tony ate in a little lunchroom at the back of the store. As Tony ate, Joe sat down next to him. Joe was 16. He had worked at Village Market for a year.

"Do you like it here so far?" Joe asked.

"Except for the can crash, everything has been great," Tony answered. "Even then, Benny made me feel like it was no big deal."

Joe leaned forward and whispered, "Benny's a good guy to know."

Just then, three other employees entered the lunchroom.

Joe glanced at them and said, "Benny's a good guy. Right, Mel?"

Melody, the tallest of the three, nodded. "Sure. A great guy," she said. But Tony saw Mel look nervously out the lunchroom door.

> **3. How do you think the other employees really feel about Benny?**

After lunch, Tony asked Benny what to do next. "Bag groceries for now," Benny answered.

"Right, boss," Tony replied.

"I like you, Tony," Benny said. "You're doing a good job."

"Benny's great," Tony thought. But he wondered if Mel really thought so.

---

explosion (ehk SPLOH zhuhn) *noun* An explosion is a sudden burst with a loud noise.

Tony's shift was over. It had been a good day. As he walked home, Tony's neighbor, Mrs. Vargas, watched him from her window. Tony liked her, even if she was a bit nosy.

"Tony's still wearing his cap and apron," she said to her husband. "He's proud of his job."

"Good," Mr. Vargas declared.

"I wonder how he'll feel when he sees what goes on at Village Market," she said.

"You don't know for sure what goes on there," Mr. Vargas said.

"I know enough to worry," she explained.

4. What do you think Mrs. Vargas is worried about?

Name _____   Date _____

Thinking About the Selection

 Fill in the circle of the correct answer.

① This story is mostly about—
   Ⓐ how Tony got his job at Village Market.
   Ⓑ Tony's first day working at Village Market.
   Ⓒ Benny's friendship with Tony, Joe, and Mel.
   Ⓓ what Mrs. Vargas thinks happens at the store.

② Tony feels nervous at the beginning of the story because—
   Ⓐ he does not trust Benny and Joe.
   Ⓑ he heard some bad news from Mrs. Vargas.
   Ⓒ this is his first day at his first job.
   Ⓓ this is the first day he met his boss.

③ How does Benny respond when Tony knocks over the cans?
   Ⓐ He says he knows it was just an accident.
   Ⓑ He tells Tony he just lost his summer job.
   Ⓒ He tells everyone that Tony did it.
   Ⓓ He laughs when a customer trips over the cans.

④ How does Tony feel at the end of his first day?
   Ⓐ nervous   Ⓒ bored
   Ⓑ upset   Ⓓ proud

⑤ Compare and contrast Tony and Benny. Describe one way in which they are alike and one way in which they are different.

_____

_____

⑥ Is Tony a good employee? Tell why you think he is or is not. Use examples from the story.

_____

WRITE ABOUT IT!

Prewriting

Name _____ Date _____

Idea Chart

In "Starting with a Bang," Tony starts his new job at Village Market, and he likes it. Have you ever had a job? Having a job means you have to give up some things, but it also means you get other things in return. Think about what is good and bad about having a job. Also think about why someone would like a job.

 Fill in the organizer chart below. Tell what is good and bad about having a job. Tell why someone would like a job.

What you give up by having a job:
1.
2.

What you get by having a job:
1.
2.

Why someone would like a job:

Overall, I think having a job is:

good / bad (circle one).

Filling out this page will help you organize your ideas before you start writing.

Unit 1: Something Rotten at Village Market
Reading Workout Book 4, SV 9781419099076

Name _____ Date _____

A Plan for Writing

Good Information

An essay gives information and ideas. An essay must have details to support the main idea.

 Write an essay to tell what is good and bad about having a job. Also tell why someone would like a job.

Tell if you think a job is good or bad.

Having a job means that you might give some things up and that you get other things in return. Overall, though, I think having a job is _____.

Tell what you give up.

Having a job means you have to give up _____
_____.

It also means giving up _____
_____.

Tell what you get.

However, having a job means you get _____
_____.

It also means getting _____
_____.

Tell why someone would like a job.

Someone would like a job because _____
_____
_____.

Writing

 Write an essay that tells what is good and bad about having a job. Also tell why someone would like a job. Give good reasons why.

www.harcourtschoolsupply.com   17   Unit 1: Something Rotten at Village Market
© Harcourt Achieve Inc. All rights reserved.   Reading Workout Book 4, SV 9781419099076

Name _____ Date _____

Strategy Workout: Fiction

Character

Readers learn about story characters by what they do and say. Authors also give details that describe how old the characters are, the way they look, or other things about them.

 In this story you learned about two main characters. Use the circles below to tell about Tony and Benny. Tell about the following things:

- how old they are
- what they look like
- what they do
- what they are like

In the circles, tell about how they are different. In the space where the circles overlap, tell about how they are alike.

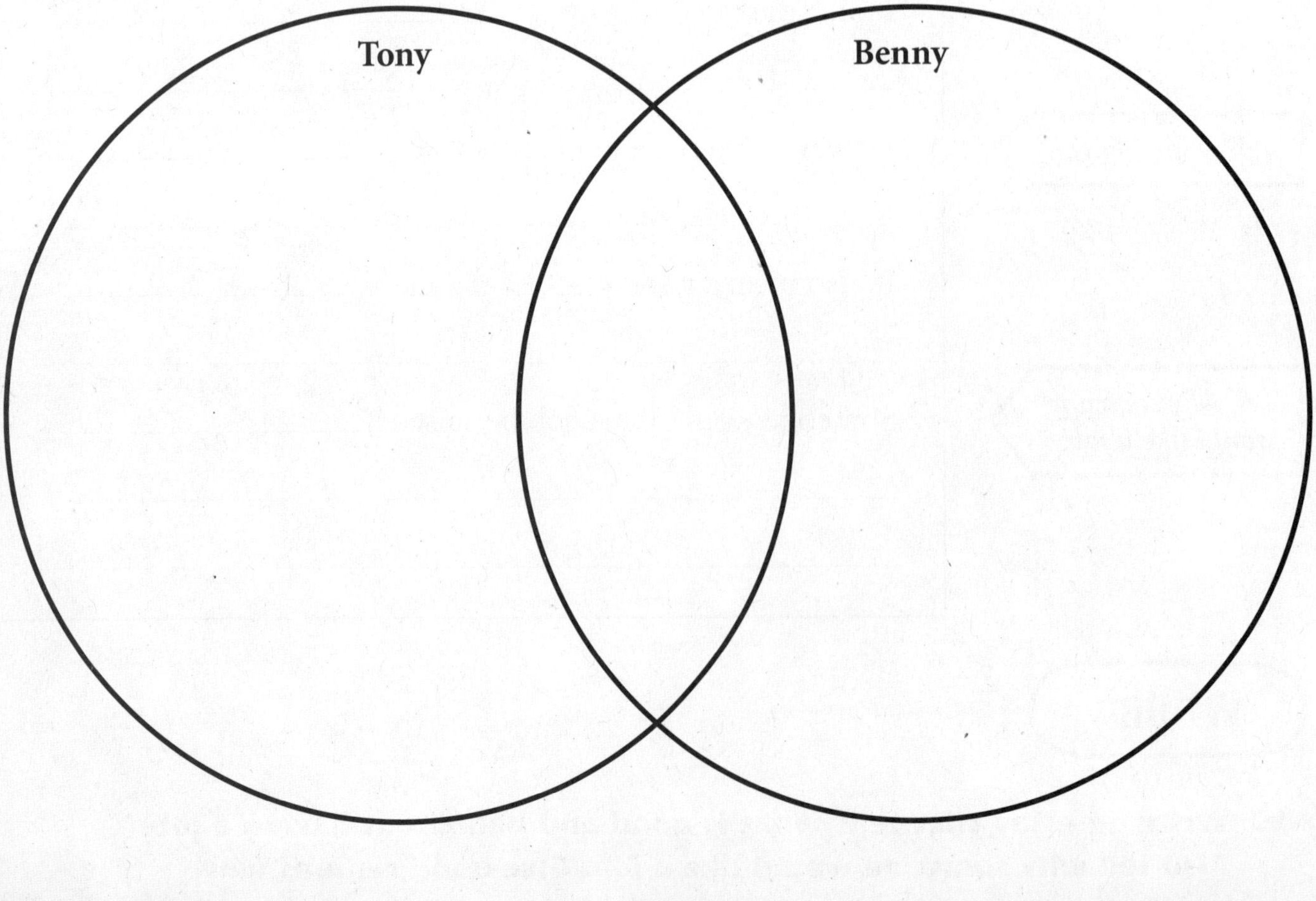

Tony   Benny

Unit 1: Something Rotten at Village Market
Reading Workout Book 4, SV 9781419099076

Name _____ Date _____

Words, Words, Words

Homonyms

Some words sound the same but have different spellings and meanings. Tony thinks that Benny is **great**. For lunch, he might **grate** some cheese to put on a pizza. **Great** and **grate** sound the same, but they are different words. These words are called *homonyms*. You can tell what a homonym means by the context, or the words around that word.

 Each pair of sentences below has two words that sound the same but have different meanings and spellings. Circle these words.

> Tony turned pale when he knocked over the cans.
> Benny helped him get a pail to clean up.
>
> ●
>
> They sold pies made by the baker.
> Tony helped customers find the things they wanted to buy.

 Circle the homonym that completes each of the sentences below.

1. Tony asked (**whether**, **weather**) he would get fired.

2. Benny treats Tony better than Tony would have (**guest**, **guessed**).

3. If Tony does a good job, he might get a (**raise**, **rays**).

4. Tony wonders if Mel really likes Benny, but he does not say this (**allowed**, **aloud**).

 Now write four sentences using the homonyms that you did not circle in the sentences above. Use one homonym in each sentence.

5. _____

6. _____

7. _____

8. _____

GETTING READY TO READ

Name _____ Date _____

Strategy: Comparing and Contrasting

People, places, things, and events can all be compared and contrasted. Authors tell how things are alike by comparing them. Authors tell how things are different by contrasting them. Authors might organize their texts by first telling you how things are similar and then telling how things are different.

 Read the passage below. Think about how the two choices are alike and how they are different.

> Many **teens** choose to go to **trade school**. If I go there, I will **accumulate** job skills. These skills will help me earn more than **minimum wage**. I could take a class on using a **camcorder**. A professional photographer would serve as my **mentor**.
>
> However, my **guardians** recommend that I go to college. There, I would learn **socialization skills** and be exposed to **unlimited** knowledge.
>
> Both choices have **benefits**. Which should I choose?

 In this passage, the writer tells about educational choices. How are these choices similar? How are they different? Write your answers in the boxes below.

How Are the Choices <u>Alike</u>?	How Are the Choices <u>Different</u>?

Comparing and contrasting will help you organize ideas and think about what you read.

Name _____ Date _____

Vocabulary Builder

The words in the box come from the passage you just read. You will see these words again in the passage you are about to read.

accumulate
benefits
~~*camcorder*~~
guardians
mentor
minimum wage
socialization skills
teens
trade school
unlimited

 Complete each sentence with one of the words. The first one has been done for you.

1. I am the word ___camcorder___. I am a camera that records movement.

2. I am the word _____. I have no boundaries.

3. I am the words _____. If you take a job, you will at least earn me.

4. I am the word _____. I am a shortened name for people who are more than 12 and less than 20 years old.

5. I am the word _____. *Advantages* is another word for me.

6. I am the words _____. I am a place to go to learn skills and practical knowledge. People might come to me instead of college.

7. I am the word _____. I advise or help someone.

8. We are the word _____. By law, we care for a child.

9. We are the words _____. We help you get along with other people.

10. I am the word _____. To gather or collect, that is me.

Purpose for Reading

Now you will read about why teenagers work. They work to help people, to meet new people, to earn money, or to do all of these things.

Why Work?

Yari Quinto sees the latest movies for free. How does she do it? On weekends and after school, the 17-year-old student works as an usher at a movie theater. She can watch films when she works. She can also bring a friend to the theater at other times and get in free.

Seeing new movies is important to Yari. She wants to be a film director. That's one reason Yari likes her job. She learns about something she loves—movies.

Working at the theater also gives Yari some independence. She has learned to manage her time and communicate well with others. She makes her own decisions about the money she earns. She has used some of her money to buy DVDs of her favorite films. She also has bought a **camcorder** to make her own movies.

> 1. What kind of job would you like to learn about? Why do you want to learn about that job?

There are other **benefits** of the job. Yari meets new people. She learns about new ideas. Her job might help her as a film director. It definitely will help her as an adult, because she is learning important **socialization skills**. She is learning how to get along with people.

---

camcorder (KAM kawrd uhr) *noun* A camcorder is a small camera that records moving images on videotape.
benefits (BEHN uh fihts) *noun* Benefits are good things a person gets as a result of something else.
socialization skills (soh shuh ly ZAY shun SKIHLZ) *noun* Socialization skills are abilities that help a person handle people and social situations.

Yari is like a lot of **teens**. Before graduating from high school, 85 percent of all teens in the United States work. Some of them work before they reach high school.

Teens work for many reasons. Wanting to become independent is one reason. A desire to make money is another one. To make sure that people are paid fairly for their work, the government sets a **minimum wage**. That means you cannot be paid less than the set amount for every hour you work.

Yari makes more than $120 a week. That's almost $500 a month for her part-time job.

2. What problems might result if there was no minimum wage law?

Spending and Saving Money

Many teens get jobs so they can buy things they want or need. They can buy items such as CDs or clothes. Their parents or **guardians** might be happy if they helped pay for their books or other school needs.

---

teens (TEENZ) *noun* Teens are people aged 13 to 19. The word *teens* is short for *teenagers*.
minimum wage (MIHN ih muhm WAYJ) *noun* Minimum wage is the least amount of money an employer can pay a person for an hour of work.
guardians (GAHRD ee uhnz) *noun* Guardians are people who are allowed by law to care for a child.

Name _____ Date _____

Have you ever dreamed of owning a car? Many items, such as cars or computers, cost a lot of money. If you want an expensive item, you might have to save money for a long time. By the end of several months, or even years, you could have enough money to buy that item. Saving money helps you learn to make wise spending choices.

Many people save money from their jobs in order to **accumulate** money for college. Others save their money so they can go to **trade school** or get other training after high school.

Getting Experience Doing What You Like

Like Yari, some teens get a job so they can use their talents or learn about something that interests them. If you like to write, you might find a job helping out at a newspaper, magazine, or book publisher. If you like cars, you might work at a mechanic's shop or for a car dealer.

Bill Gates helped start the computer software company Microsoft®. He began working with computers as a teen. A company hired him to find out what was wrong with its computer system. The company didn't pay him in cash. Instead, it gave him **unlimited** time on the company's computers. Gates got the experience he needed to start Microsoft seven years later.

> **3. Why do you think the author told us how Bill Gates got started?**

accumulate (uh KYOOM yoo layt) *verb* To accumulate means "to gather."
trade school (TRAYD SKOOL) *noun* Trade school is where you go to learn a skill, such as how to fix cars.
unlimited (uhn LIHM iht ihd) *adjective* Unlimited means "without limits or boundaries."

Name _____   Date _____

Reasons for Getting a Job

Reasons	Benefits
Independence	Learn to make decisions; learn to manage your time and money; learn to ask for days off, raises, and new work duties.
Money	Be able to buy things for yourself and your family; be able to save for items you want; be able to save for college.
Experience	Find out what you like to do and what you're good at; gain experience and confidence.
Community	Meet friends outside of school; meet people who can help you get into college or find a job; meet people different from you.

Another way to get experience is to volunteer. When you volunteer, you work without getting paid. Instead, you learn about a new field. If you like to work with animals, you could volunteer at your city's Humane Society.

Name _____ Date _____

Getting to Know Other People

Another reason to get a job is to make friends outside of your school or neighborhood. You might meet people with the same interests as you. You might also meet people you find interesting because they are different from yourself. They might be older than you, or they might speak a different language.

You might even find a **mentor**. This is someone who spends time with you, teaches you, and gives you advice. A mentor might help you apply for college or give you a full-time job when you finish school.

There are many reasons to work. The most important reason might not be to make money. You might work because you want to make your world a better place. Working can teach you new ways to use your talents.

4. **What do you think is the author's viewpoint on working teenagers?**

_____

_____

_____

_____

_____

---

mentor (MEHN tuhr) *noun* A mentor is someone who advises and helps another person.

Name _____   Date _____

Thinking About the Selection

 Fill in the circle of the correct answer.

1. The author's purpose for writing this passage was to—
   Ⓐ entertain readers with stories about work.
   Ⓑ convince readers not to work.
   Ⓒ give readers reasons for working.
   Ⓓ tell readers how to get a job.

2. One way a volunteer job is different from other jobs is that you—
   Ⓐ get to do work in which you are interested.
   Ⓑ do not get paid for your work.
   Ⓒ will meet many people at work.
   Ⓓ work with animals instead of people.

3. This passage says that a mentor might help you—
   Ⓐ plan your future.   Ⓒ do your homework.
   Ⓑ improve your health.   Ⓓ make more friends.

4. How many students work before they finish high school?
   Ⓐ very few (about 10%)   Ⓒ half (about 50%)
   Ⓑ some (about 30%)   Ⓓ most (about 85%)

5. Why does the government set a minimum amount that you should get paid for working?

   _____
   _____

6. What are two of the ways that working can be good for teenagers?

   _____
   _____

WRITE ABOUT IT!

Prewriting

Name _____ Date _____

Planning Chart

In "Why Work?" you learn many reasons why it is good for teenagers to have jobs. Think of a job that you might like to have right now. Why do you want it? Why would you be good at it?

➡ **Fill in the chart below. Tell about a job that you would like. Tell why you would be good at it and give examples. This will help to show that you should get the job.**

A job I would like: _____

_____

Why I would like this job: _____

_____

_____

Why I would be good at this job:	Examples that show how I would be good in each way:
1.	1.
2.	2.

Filling out this page will help you organize your ideas before you start writing.

Name _____ Date _____

A Plan for Writing

I Am the Person for This Job

Sometimes you need to write a business letter in order to do or get something.

➡ **Write a letter about a job you want. Use ideas from your chart.**

Your Name, Street, City, State, ZIP Code go here

Today's Date goes here

Person's Name, Place of Business, Address, City, State, ZIP Code go here

Greeting

Body Paragraph 1: Tell what job you want.

Body Paragraph 2: Tell why you would be good.

Body Paragraph 3: Tell why and how much you want the job.

Closing

Signature

Dear _____,

I would like to _____.

This letter tells why I think I would be good at this job.

I would be good at this job because _____.

An example of this is _____.

I would also be good at this job because _____.

An example of this is _____.

Please select me for this job because _____.

Sincerely,

_____

Writing

➡ **Write a business letter on a separate sheet of paper. Tell why you should be hired for a job. Use the plan above to help you.**

Name _____ Date _____

Strategy Workout: Nonfiction

Research Skills and Strategies

The books and stories you read can change the way you think or act. This selection might have made you want to look for a job. There are many different places you could look to find information about jobs.

> **Classified Advertisements**: This is a section of the newspaper. It is a place for employers to put information about available jobs in your city or town.
>
> **Internet**: The Internet has information about jobs around the country. For example, the Internet would be a good place to find a list of summer camps.
>
> **Job Listings**: There might be flyers posted at your school, library, church, or community center. These are usually from people in your neighborhood who want help in their homes or taking care of their yard.
>
> **Library**: The library has books about how to apply for jobs.
>
> **Telephone Book**: The business pages of the telephone book might help. If you know you are interested in working at a nursery, for example, you could look up nurseries in the yellow pages.

 Answer the following questions by writing the best place to look for this information.

1. Where can I find information about jobs around the country? _____

2. Where can I go for help on how to write a job application? _____

3. Where can I look to find a lawn-care job in my neighborhood? _____

4. Where can I look to find pet stores and animal shelters in my town? _____

5. Where can I look to find a list of available jobs in my town? _____

Name _____ Date _____

Words, Words, Words

Synonyms and Antonyms

Synonyms are words with the same or almost the same meaning. Antonyms are words with opposite or nearly opposite meanings. Thinking about synonyms and antonyms when you read can help you understand what you are reading.

 Circle the antonym that best fits the meaning of each sentence. Use what you learned in the reading passage to help you choose which word to circle.

1. Having a job can have (**few, many**) advantages for a young person.

2. A working teen will learn how to get along (**well, poorly**) with others.

3. A job might also help a teen (**earn, lose**) money.

4. Having the right job could be a (**good, bad**) way to help get future jobs.

5. Working teens might also get to (**forget, know**) different people.

 In the sentences below, think of a synonym for each underlined word. Write the synonym on the line.

6. A job with computers might be good for a person who is timid.
   _____

7. A job at the zoo might be ideal if you love animals. _____

8. Someone who likes to work where it is silent might want to work at the library.
   _____

9. Someone who likes to work where it is noisy might want to work at a music store.
   _____

10. If you like working outside, a job mowing yards might be right for you.
    _____

GETTING READY TO READ

Name _____ Date _____

Strategy: Identifying Cause and Effect

When we read, we think about why things happened and what might happen next. Why something happens is the cause. What happens as a result is the effect. When you read, if you ask yourself *why*, *how*, and *what if*, you are asking yourself questions about causes and effects.

 Read the passage below. Think about what happens and why.

> Science class is cool. I don't say that **sarcastically**. We watched a movie about how two astronauts **salvaged** a satellite in space. The **video** screen showed how one astronaut used a robot to **retrieve** a **solar panel**. Another astronaut was there to **monitor** his efforts. Her presence was **crucial** to make sure he didn't float away because of the weak **gravitational** pull in space. We also learned about the flight **simulations** that astronauts use when they train. The simulations are like **virtual-reality** experiences! How cool!

 This passage tells about why the author thinks that science class is cool. What causes the author to think that science is cool?

The author thinks science class is cool because:

1. _____
   _____

2. _____
   _____

Sometimes a story tells you why events happen. Sometimes you have to think on your own about why events happened and what their results might be. Either way, you are thinking about causes and effects.

Asking yourself *why*, *how*, and *what if* will help you understand what you read.

Name _____ Date _____

Vocabulary Builder

The words in the box come from the passage you just read. You will see these words again in the play you are about to read.

Choose a word from the box to complete each sentence. Write the letters of the word on the blanks. The first word has been done for you. When you are finished, the letters in the circles will make three words. These words will tell you the setting for the play you will read.

virtual-reality
retrieve
solar panel
~~monitor~~
simulations
gravitational
sarcastically
video
salvaged
crucial

1. To m(o)n i t o r means "to watch over and to make sure everything is going smoothly."

2. Every choice he makes in the emergency room is _ _(_)_ _ _ _.

3. I threw the ball and waited for my dog to _ _(_)_ _ _ _ it.

4. Earth's _ _ _ _(_)_ _ _ _ _ _ _ pull is what keeps us from floating out into space.

5. The pilot learned to fly using _ _ _ _ _ _ _ _ _(_).

6. I (_)_ _ _ _ _ _ _ a few books from the bottom of the heap.

7. The _ _ _ _ _ (_)_ _ _ _ gives us heat from the sun.

8. _ _ _ _ _ _(_)_ _ _ _ _ _ _ _ games make you feel as if you are really flying a plane or driving a race car.

9. My brother said that I look like a movie star, but he said that _ _ _(_)_ _ _ _ _ _ _ _ _.

10. In class we watched a movie on the _ _ _(_)_ screen.

Answer: _ _ _ _ _ _ _ _ _ _ _

Name _____ Date _____

Purpose for Reading

Now you are going to read a play about a spaceship in the future. Will the three teenagers complete the job?

In the Virtual-Reality Room

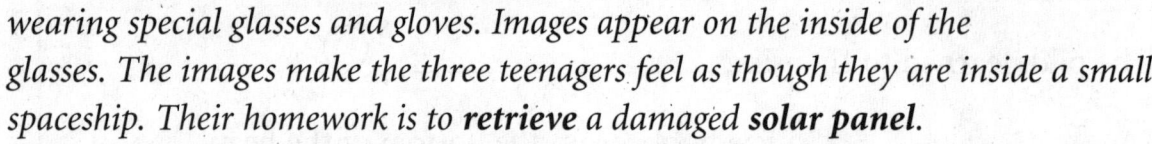

This play takes place many years in the future. Forty people of all ages are traveling on a spaceship from Moon Base toward the planet Venus. Their mission is to build a new space station near the planet. Everyone is expected to help.

Alex, Maria, and Greg are working on their **virtual-reality** homework. They are wearing special glasses and gloves. Images appear on the inside of the glasses. The images make the three teenagers feel as though they are inside a small spaceship. Their homework is to **retrieve** a damaged **solar panel**.

Alex and Greg are operating robot arms. Their job is to grab the solar panel. Maria is piloting the spacecraft. Her job is to **monitor** what is happening around their spaceship.

    ALEX   We're ready to attach the panel, Greg. All clear, Maria?

    MARIA   All clear. Wait—oh, no!

---

virtual-reality (VUR choo uhl ree AL uh tee) *adjective* Virtual-reality is images of a location or situation that appear on a screen. They seem to be real, but they are actually created by a computer. You can work with these images using special equipment.

retrieve (rih TREEV) *verb* To retrieve something means "to get it back."

solar panel (SOH luhr PAN uhl) *noun* A solar panel is a surface that changes sunlight into electricity.

monitor (MAHN ih tuhr) *verb* To monitor means "to watch carefully."

Name _____ Date _____

Suddenly the spaceship starts to shake violently. It is caught in a meteor shower. Alex loses his grip on the robot arm and drops the panel. A red light begins to flash on a screen in front of Maria.

VR-146 Emergency!

ALEX (*nervously*) We know it's an emergency!

VR-146 Emergency!

MARIA (*joking*) Is there an echo in here?

GREG (*angrily*) This isn't a game, Maria.

MARIA (*arguing*) Yes, it is. These **simulations** are just like games, only with an extra kick, like a meteor shower.

GREG Just do your job, Maria, or get off my team.

---

1. Why do you think Greg was angry with Maria?

MARIA *Your* team?

VR-146 Emergency! You have 30 seconds before you enter the sun's **gravitational** field.

ALEX (*scared*) Stop fighting, you two. We're going to lose the panel!

GREG Maria! Move us closer to the panel!

MARIA (*sarcastically*) Yes, sir!

---

simulations (sihm yoo LAY shuhnz) *noun* Simulations are situations created by a computer so you can practice doing something that you will do later for real.

gravitational (grav ih TAY shuhn uhl) *adjective* Something that is gravitational pulls other things toward it very strongly.

sarcastically (sahr KAS tihk lee) *adverb* When you say something sarcastically, you usually mean the opposite of what you say.

VR-146 You have 15 seconds.

GREG Alex, I'm pushing the panel back toward your robot arm now.

ALEX (*concentrating hard*) OK. I have it.

VR-146 . . . 10 . . . 9 . . .

GREG Let's pull it in together. Steady.

VR-146 . . . 6 . . . 5 . . .

GREG The panel is locked on! Maria, get us out of here!

MARIA You don't have to ask twice!

VR-146 . . . 2 . . . 1 . . .

The engines roar as the virtual-reality spaceship speeds away from the meteor shower. The room lights up. The simulation is over. A large **video** *screen comes on, and Mr. Collins appears. The three teenagers gather in front of the screen. A camera on top of the screen sends their images back to Mr. Collins, who is at Moon Base.*

MR. C. I'm a little disappointed in today's exercise.

---

2. Why do you think Mr. Collins was disappointed?

GREG But we **salvaged** the panel!

MR. C. Yes, Greg, but you forgot to check the robot arms before starting your mission. Alex, you lost control too easily. It can get rough up there.

ALEX Yes, sir.

---

video (VIHD ee oh) *adjective* Video is what you see on a computer or television screen.
salvaged (SAL vihjd) *verb* To have salvaged something is to have saved or rescued it.

MR. C. (*sternly*) Maria, this is not a game. The work you'll be doing on the space station is **crucial**. Moon Base is depending on the success of your mission.

MARIA (*mumbling*) I didn't—

MR. C. Did someone say something? I didn't quite hear—

ALEX (*quickly*) I said, "We'll do better next time, sir."

MR. C. I hope so, Alex. You need to be able to work together as a team. Moon Base out.

---

3. What do you think the three need to do first to work together as a team?

The screen goes blank.

MARIA These simulations are a drag.

ALEX You heard Mr. Collins. This is important!

MARIA Do you really think we'll be picking up broken solar panels all by ourselves? If it's so important, the adults will do it. They won't trust us with anything crucial.

---

crucial (KROO shuhl) *adjective* Something that is crucial is very important.

Greg and Maria start to leave the room. Alex stays behind, staring at the blank video screen.

MARIA   Are you coming, Alex?

ALEX   I was just thinking . . .

GREG   Now you're thinking? It's time to start having fun.

ALEX   (*ignoring Greg*) Sometimes I wish someone would tell us what's really going on.

MARIA   What do you mean?

ALEX   Well, what are we going to use to build the space station? Will we try to mine the surface of Venus? Do you ever feel like the adults are keeping secrets?

MARIA   It is pretty insulting that they won't tell us.

---

4. Why do you think Maria feels insulted?

GREG   Maybe they don't know themselves.

MARIA   (*sarcastically*) You mean the adults don't know everything?

ALEX   I just think this mission is more dangerous than the adults let on.

Alex follows Greg and Maria out the door. A small red light in the ceiling flashes. It is a hidden camera. Someone is watching.

Name _____ Date _____

Thinking About the Selection

 Fill in the circle of the correct answer.

1. Why are these teenagers traveling to the planet Venus?
   - Ⓐ to find a better place to live
   - Ⓑ to build a space station
   - Ⓒ for a vacation
   - Ⓓ for a school field trip

2. Why is Greg angry with Maria?
   - Ⓐ She is not taking the work seriously.
   - Ⓑ She is taking the work too seriously.
   - Ⓒ She and Alex keep arguing.
   - Ⓓ She will not let him play the game.

3. What does Mr. Collins want the three teenagers to learn?
   - Ⓐ how to repair the virtual-reality room
   - Ⓑ how to crack computer codes
   - Ⓒ how to build a solar panel
   - Ⓓ how to work well together

4. At the end of this play, Alex thinks—
   - Ⓐ it's time to start having fun.
   - Ⓑ their mission is dangerous.
   - Ⓒ the adults don't know everything.
   - Ⓓ someone is watching with a hidden camera.

5. How are Maria and Greg alike?
   _____
   _____

6. What is Alex worried about at the end of the selection?
   _____
   _____

WRITE ABOUT IT!

Prewriting

Name _____ Date _____

Idea Chart

In "In the Virtual-Reality Room," Alex, Greg, and Maria have to retrieve a damaged solar panel in a simulation. They save the panel, but they do not work together well. Think about something that you can do with a partner. Think about how you would instruct your partner to work with you.

 Fill in the chart below. Tell what the three main steps are, and write details about how to do each step. Tell what you do and what your partner does.

Something I Can Do: _____

Why I Need Someone's Help to Do This: _____
_____

STEP 1	STEP 2	STEP 3
What I Do	What I Do	What I Do
What You Do	What You Do	What You Do

Filling out this page will help you organize your ideas before you start writing.

Name _____ Date _____

A Plan for Writing

How To

Instructions tell how to do something. Instructions must be clear and in the correct order so that someone can learn from them.

 Write instructions to tell someone how you would work together to do something. Use ideas from your chart.

What you can do

I know how to _____. I need to do this with someone because _____
_____.

Here is how we would do this.

Step 1 with details

First I _____.

While I do this, you _____.

Step 2 with details

Next I _____
_____.

While I do this, you _____
_____.

Step 3 with details

Finally I _____
_____.

While I do this, you _____.

Writing

 Write instructions to tell someone how to help you do something. Use the plan above to help you write. Tell what you will do. Tell what the other person will do. Write your instructions on a separate sheet of paper.

Name _____   Date _____

Strategy Workout: Fiction

Setting

The place where a story or play happens is called the *setting*. This play is set in a time and place in which you have never been. You can still picture and imagine what it would be like.

 Think about where "In the Virtual-Reality Room" takes place. Draw a picture of the place where these characters are living. Then complete the sentences below to tell about your picture. Use details from the story.

[Drawing box]

1. The year is _____.

2. The place is _____.

3. My picture shows _____.

www.harcourtschoolsupply.com
© Harcourt Achieve Inc. All rights reserved.

Unit 1: Space Play
Reading Workout Book 4, SV 9781419099076

Name _____ Date _____

Words, Words, Words

Figurative Language

It is important that the characters in a story or play seem real. Sometimes this means that the authors will have the characters use idioms or slang. Idioms are phrases that have special meanings, such as *He is a couch potato*. Words in an idiom take on a different meaning when they are used together. Slang is language that people might use with their friends in a casual way, such as *She is all that*.

➡ **Maria uses figurative language in the play. What is she really saying?**

1. What Maria says: "You don't have to ask twice!"

   What she means: _____

2. What Maria says: "These simulations are just like games, only with an extra kick, like a meteor shower."

   What she means: _____

3. What Maria says: "These simulations are a drag."

   What she means: _____

➡ **The sentences below describe what happened in the play. What does each underlined idiom in the sentence mean?**

4. The three teenagers were all in the same boat; they had to finish the assignment.

   _____

5. They worked against the clock to get the panel.

   _____

6. If they had failed, they would have been in the doghouse.

   _____

7. They went down to the wire to complete the job.

   _____

8. Alex thinks he needs to keep an eye on the situation on the spaceship.

   _____

GETTING READY TO READ

Strategy: Identifying Cause and Effect

When something happens, we can usually think of reasons why it happens. Why something happens is the *cause*. What happens as a result is the *effect*. We can usually see how one event causes another event to occur. Sometimes authors tell us causes and effects. Sometimes we have to figure them out.

 Read the passage below. Think about what happens and why.

> U.S. competition to **overtake** other countries' triumphs has led to **significant achievement**. In the 1950s, spaceflight was **science fiction**. Then the Soviet Union sent **modules** with **cosmonauts** into space. The United States knew that the race to space was on. The country soon created the **complex technology** to land a man on the moon.
>
> Knowledge is **expandable**. **Mankind** always wants to know more. There are always new areas of Earth and space sciences to explore. Who knows what information we will have in another fifty years?

 Think about the passage. What causes and effects did you learn about? Write about them in the chart below.

The Event That Is the Effect	The Event That Is the Cause
The United States raced to make the technology to put a man on the moon.	This race started because:
In fifty years we will probably have new information we cannot even imagine now.	We will probably have new information because:

Thinking about causes and effects helps you understand why events happen the way they do. This can help you understand what you read, especially in history or science.

Name _____ Date _____

Vocabulary Builder

The words in the box come from the passage you just read. You will see these words again in the passage you are about to read.

 Write the correct word in each sentence. This will help you think about the words before you begin reading. The first one has been done for you.

> achievement
> complex
> cosmonauts
> expandable
> mankind
> modules
> overtake
> ~~science fiction~~
> significant
> technology

① I like to read __science fiction__ about imaginary worlds in space.

② _____ are sections or parts of a bigger thing.

③ It took me several hours to finish the _____ job of assembling the bike.

④ Because I am a woman, I wonder why all humans are called _____.

⑤ He included all of the _____ details in his history paper.

⑥ I cannot imagine life without the invention of _____ such as computers.

⑦ Jill was first in the race until Kira started to _____ her.

⑧ Winning the race was Kira's greatest _____ as a runner.

⑨ Russian or Soviet astronauts are called _____.

⑩ His English teacher told him to think of his paper as _____ and to add new words and ideas to it.

Purpose for Reading

Now you are going to read about the U.S. race to explore space. Read on to find out how the race started and what happened next.

Name _____   Date _____

The Race to Space

A rocket taking off for outer space is a common event these days. However, space travel was just **science fiction** only fifty or sixty years ago. It took competition between two countries to turn science fiction into fact.

The Cold War

In the 1950s, the United States and the Soviet Union were in a power struggle. (Present-day Russia was part of the Soviet Union.) This time was known as the Cold War. The two countries were not really at war, but they were very suspicious of each other. Each country wanted to be the first to explore space.

> 1. Why do you think each country wanted to be first to explore space?

The Soviets Were First

On October 4, 1957, the Soviets launched *Sputnik 1*. *Sputnik* means "satellite" in Russian. *Sputnik 1* was the first satellite successfully launched into orbit around Earth.

One month later, the Soviets sent a dog into space on board *Sputnik 2*. *Laika*, which means "barker" in Russian, was the first living creature sent into space.

> **science fiction** (SY uhns FIHK shuhn) *noun* Science fiction refers to imaginative stories that are set in the future, in outer space, on another planet, or that include scientific themes.

The Soviets then had another **significant** first. On April 12, 1961, Yuri Gagarin made a full orbit around Earth on board a Soviet rocket.

Man on the Moon

The United States wanted to catch up to and **overtake** the Soviet Union in the space race. This competition was driven by more than national pride. The U.S. government worried that the Soviets might use their space **technology** as a weapon against the people of the United States.

The National Aeronautics and Space Administration (NASA) was created in October 1958. Its official mission was to plan and carry out space activities. Its real mission was to beat the Soviets to the moon.

In 1961, President John F. Kennedy told the U.S. people he wanted to send astronauts to the moon and then return them safely home. It took almost 10 years to do it. On July 20, 1969, U.S. astronaut Neil Armstrong became the first person to set foot on the moon. When he climbed down the ladder onto the moon, Armstrong said, "That's one small step for a man, one giant leap for **mankind**."

Armstrong and another *Apollo 11* astronaut, Edwin "Buzz" Aldrin, Jr., walked on the moon. Millions of people around the world watched them on television. The 2 men planted a U.S. flag on the moon. That showed the world that the United States was the new leader in space.

This **achievement** captured people's imaginations. Suddenly space exploration held all kinds of wonderful possibilities.

---

significant (sihg NIHF uh kuhnt) *adjective* Significant means "important."
overtake (oh vuhr TAYK) *verb* To overtake is to catch up with and pass someone with whom you're racing.
technology (tehk NAHL uh jee) *noun* Technology is the science and study of tools and machines and their use.
mankind (man KYND) *noun* Mankind is all human beings.
achievement (uh CHEEV muhnt) *noun* An achievement is something that somebody has succeeded in doing, usually by hard work.

Name _____   Date _____

2. How do you think people felt after they watched Aldrin and Armstrong walking on the moon?

First Space Stations

The first space stations were small laboratories that orbited Earth.

Salyut

Salyut 1 was the world's first space station. The Soviet Union launched it on April 9, 1971. The first crew went by rocket to the space station 3 days later, but they could not open *Salyut's* hatch. They returned to Earth without having entered the space station.

The second *Salyut* crew got into the space station and stayed for 24 days. As the 3 **cosmonauts** returned to Earth, a valve opened, and the air inside the spacecraft escaped. The men were not wearing spacesuits to help them breathe. They died from a lack of oxygen. After that accident, all cosmonauts wore spacesuits when traveling to and from the space station.

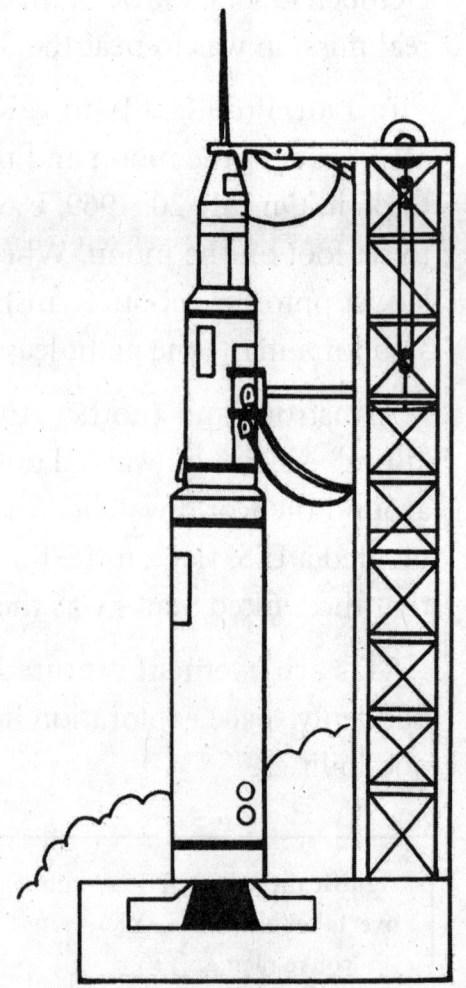

cosmonauts (KAHZ muh nawts) *noun* Cosmonauts are astronauts in the Soviet or Russian space programs.

3. Why do accidents sometimes cause changes in how things are done? What is another example of a time when an accident caused something to change?

Skylab

The U.S. space station, *Skylab*, was launched in May 1973. It was more than 3 times larger than *Salyut*. It weighed about 100 tons. *Skylab* was damaged as it went into orbit. NASA sent a team of 3 astronauts to fix the space station.

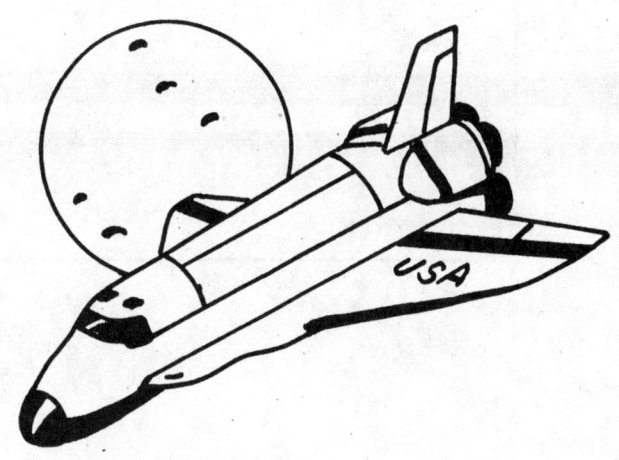

The astronauts made the repairs while *Skylab* orbited Earth. This mission showed that **complex** construction tasks could be done in space. *Skylab* missions later proved that humans could live and work in space for months at a time.

---

complex (kahm PLEHKS) *adjective* Complex means "complicated, or not simple."

Mir

The Soviets launched *Mir* in February 1986. *Mir* means "peace" in Russian. *Mir* cosmonauts became the first humans to spend more than a year in space.

Mir was the first space station designed to be **expandable**. It was made up of different pieces called **modules**. New modules were added to the space station over time. This gave the cosmonauts more room to live and work.

The early space stations *Salyut*, *Skylab*, and *Mir* are no longer in orbit.

> **4. What do you think caused NASA to believe that astronauts could put modules together in space?**

---

expandable (ehk SPAND uh buhl) *adjective* Something is expandable if it can be made larger.
modules (MAHJ oolz) *noun* Modules are sections or units of a larger thing.

Name _____ Date _____

Thinking About the Selection

➡️ **Fill in the circle of the correct answer.**

1. This passage is mostly about—
   Ⓐ why the United States and Soviet Union competed.
   Ⓑ how the technology was developed to send a man to the moon.
   Ⓒ the early history of space travel between the 1950s and 1980s.
   Ⓓ the development of space stations for people to live in space.

2. According to this passage, one reason the United States wanted to send a person into space was because it—
   Ⓐ was trying to do it before the Soviet Union did.
   Ⓑ wanted to catch up to and beat the Soviet Union.
   Ⓒ did not have any more science to study on Earth.
   Ⓓ wanted to prove that Earth was round, not flat.

3. The first living creature sent to space was a—
   Ⓐ dog.   Ⓒ frog.
   Ⓑ person.   Ⓓ cockroach.

4. The author probably wrote this passage to—
   Ⓐ compare the Soviet and U.S. achievements in space.
   Ⓑ tell about how and why space travel became reality.
   Ⓒ convince people about the importance of space travel.
   Ⓓ entertain readers with imaginary stories about space.

5. Why was Neil Armstrong's first walk on the moon so important?
   _____
   _____

6. What details in this passage show that people might live in space someday?
   _____
   _____

WRITE ABOUT IT!

Name _____ Date _____

Prewriting

Filling out this page will help you put your ideas in order before you start writing.

Idea Chart

"The Race to Space" tells about the important things that happened while the United States and the Soviet Union tried to explore space. Each country wanted to be faster and better than the other.

Think about an experience or relationship you have had with another person. What were the main or most important things that happened in the experience or relationship? In what order did they happen?

 Fill out the chart below. Tell what happened. In the right column, write the number 1, 2, or 3 to tell the order in which each thing happened.

This is about: _____

What Happened	The Order in Which It Happened

www.harcourtschoolsupply.com
© Harcourt Achieve Inc. All rights reserved.

Unit 1: The Moon and Beyond
Reading Workout Book 4, SV 9781419099076

Name _____ Date _____

A Plan for Writing

Summary of Someone Else and Me

A summary tells only the main or important things. It is much shorter than a story. It does not have all the details that a story has.

 Write a summary of an experience or relationship you had with another person. Use the ideas from your chart.

Paragraph 1: Tell what happened first.

This is a summary of _____.

First _____
_____
_____
_____

Paragraph 2: Tell what happened next.

Then _____
_____
_____
_____

Paragraph 3: Tell what happened last.

Finally _____
_____
_____
_____

Writing

 Write a summary about an experience or relationship with someone. Use the plan above to help you. Describe only the three most important parts of what you did. Write your summary on a separate sheet of paper.

Name _____ Date _____

Strategy Workout: Nonfiction

Pictures, Charts, and Graphs

When you read books about science or history, there are usually pictures, charts, and graphs that give you more information. Authors also use pictures, charts, and graphs to give you information in a way that might be easier to understand than words alone would be.

The passage you read had different pictures. Now you have a chance to add your own timeline and picture to the story.

 On the timeline, list three important events in space exploration that you learned in the passage.

1950 _____

_____ 1955

1960 _____

_____ 1965

1970 _____

_____ 1975

1980 _____

_____ 1985

1990 _____

 Draw a picture in the frame of some part of the selection that you read.

Name _____   Date _____

Words, Words, Words

Using Context Clues

One way to understand a new word is to use context clues. These are words in a story that can help you figure out a new word's meaning. Context clues might be in the same sentence or in the sentences before and after the word.

 Read the following sentences. Then match each underlined word to its meaning. Last, tell what context clues helped you learn each word's meaning.

> In the space race, the Soviets were the United States' <u>primary</u> opponents. The Soviet Union was the country closest to getting to outer space first.
>
> When the Soviet Union put a man in space, people of the United States <u>faced</u> even more pressure. Before then, U.S. citizens may have wanted to go to space, but they might not have felt it was so important. Now the race was real.
>
> Everyone watched in <u>disbelief</u> as Neil Armstrong walked on the moon. It was hard to believe that a man was really walking on the moon!

 Match each word with its meaning. Write the letter of the definition next to the word.

1. primary _____   a. not thinking something was true

2. faced _____   b. first or most important

3. disbelief _____   c. met with

 Tell what words from the sentences are context clues. The first one has been done for you.

Word	Context Clues
primary	4. *the country closest to getting to outer space first*
faced	5.
disbelief	6.

Take a Stand—Wrap-Up

What a Difference a Year Makes

"I wonder what it'll be like," my best friend, Felicia, said. She and I were standing in my bathroom, getting ready for our school's annual dance. Felicia had been sick last year and had to miss the dance. She was really excited about going this year.

"Well, if it is anything like last year's dance, don't expect too much," I answered.

"Oh, Josie, cheer up. It's going to be fun," Felicia said. She carefully placed a glittering red clip in her dark hair.

> **1. Do you think they will have fun at the dance? What makes you think they will or will not?**

I had good reason for being negative. Last year's dance was a disaster. Felicia had been sick, and Brittany hadn't moved to town yet. I guess I could have stayed home, but I knew that Mark Garrison was going to be there. I thought he was the cutest boy in school, and I would have given anything to dance with him. I ended up going with my older sister, who ditched me as soon as we got to the school.

There I was, standing by myself against the cafeteria wall. I had never been so nervous! Everyone else was too nervous to dance, as well. That's why my next move was a complete surprise to everyone, including me. After having stood around for about an hour, I gathered all of my courage and walked right up to Mark. I said, "Hi," in the perkiest tone I could manage. And he didn't say a word. He just stared at me. After several seconds of dead silence, I crawled away. What had I been thinking? It took me months just to be able to face him in the halls after that.

"Josie!" Felicia said. I snapped back to the present. "Are you thinking about last year again? Just forget about it *and* Mark. Hurry up and get dressed. Can you zip me up first, though?"

She spun around in her red dress, happily fluffing the skirt. She checked her reflection from all sides. The doorbell rang, and a few seconds later our friend Brittany bounced into the bathroom.

"Hey, girls! Oh, Felicia, you look great! Josie, aren't you dressed yet?" Brittany dropped her backpack on the floor. Her blond ponytail gleamed in the light as she slid in front of the mirror. I slipped into my dress and walked across the bathroom like a model, causing Felicia to giggle.

"Felicia, I love your dress. Red is definitely you," Brittany said. "Josie—good choice with black."

"Thanks," I said. Brittany's dress was frosty blue with fake diamonds along the thin straps. She even had a matching blue purse.

"I hope this year's dance is better than last year's," I said, smoothing my hair. "Hardly anyone danced."

"Of course we'll dance, Josie. Anyway, if no one goes onto the dance floor, *I'll* just go out there. Then everybody will start dancing," Brittany said.

Felicia rolled her eyes and looked over at me.

"Oh really? We'll see about that," I said.

> **2. Which character do you think is the leader of the group? Tell why you think that.**

An hour later, we walked into the school cafeteria. Kids were all dressed up and looking nervous. Blue and silver balloons danced along the ceiling. The lights were low, and piles of treats covered the snack table.

We eventually made our way around the cafeteria, sampling snacks and punch. Brittany and Felicia pointed out other girls' dresses they especially liked, and we chatted with our friends. Music was playing, but no one was dancing. I scanned the walls and saw Mark Garrison talking with his friends. He turned his head toward me, but I quickly grabbed Felicia's arm.

"Let's go get more punch," I said, pulling her with me. Every now and then, one of my favorite songs came on. The music drew me toward the floor, but I just couldn't bring myself to go out there alone. The boys watched as girls passed by on the way to the restroom. From what I could tell, there were probably more girls in the restroom than in the cafeteria. Occasionally, a few people wandered out onto the floor for a few minutes, but nothing could keep them out there. It looked like this dance was going to be a repeat of last year.

"OK, ladies and gentlemen," the DJ's voice boomed, "let's get out on the floor and have some fun!" The DJ sounded like he was having more fun by himself than all the kids combined. He played another slow love song. The minutes ticked by painfully. Every single person seemed glued to the wall.

"Well, Brittany, go on out there. We're waiting," Felicia said. She gave Brittany a little push. Brittany's eyes opened wide with fear.

I watched the other kids as they looked around. What were they waiting for? Then it hit me. What was *I* waiting for? It shouldn't matter that no one else was dancing. I loved to dance, and I liked the music the DJ was playing. Besides, someone had to do something to get this party going—it might as well be me.

"I'll be back," I called over my shoulder. I marched over to the DJ's booth, feeling exposed as everyone's eyes followed me. I requested a bunch of fast songs, and the DJ said he would play them.

Wow! I felt great. I would never have done that last year. What a difference a year makes. I went to my friends and pulled them onto the dance floor.

3. How do you think Josie is different from the way she was last year?

Name _____ Date _____

"OK, girls, let's dance—it's now or never," I said. They looked scared, but they came with me. As Brittany and Felicia left the safety of the wall, they pulled several more girls with them. Now we had a group of girls dancing in a sea of emptiness. We tried not to notice everybody staring at us.

"Keep dancing and be brave!" I said. We smiled at each other as we danced. Very slowly, more and more kids peeled themselves away from the walls. Some joined our circle, and others made their own groups. We were finally having a real dance! Felicia and Brittany laughed as they looked around. Then someone bumped my arm. It was Mark!

"Oops—sorry," he grinned. "Can I join in?"

Immediately, Felicia slid away from me, making room for Mark.

"Sure, there's plenty of room," I said, my heart jumping for joy. This dance wasn't so bad after all.

4. Why do you think Mark asked to join in?

Name _____   Date _____

Take a Stand—Wrap-Up

 Fill in the circle of the correct answer.

① This story is mostly about—
  Ⓐ why fast songs are more fun than slow songs.
  Ⓑ what to wear to a school dance.
  Ⓒ why Josie had a bad time at last year's dance.
  Ⓓ a girl who decides to have fun at a dance.

② How does Felicia feel at the beginning of the story?
  Ⓐ excited   Ⓒ tired
  Ⓑ nervous   Ⓓ bored

③ What happens last in this story?
  Ⓐ Josie's friend is sick and cannot go to the dance.
  Ⓑ Mark asks if he can dance.
  Ⓒ Josie asks Mark to dance with her.
  Ⓓ The DJ plays a slow love song.

④ How is this year's dance different from last year's dance?
  Ⓐ Josie has a boyfriend this year.
  Ⓑ Josie dances and has fun this year.
  Ⓒ Josie had more fun last year.
  Ⓓ Josie only danced with her friends last year.

⑤ What does Josie do differently this year than last year? Give examples from the story to support your answer.

_____

_____

⑥ How does Josie feel at the end of the story? Explain what makes you think that.

_____

_____

Name _____ Date _____

Take a Stand—Wrap-Up

Lend a Hand

An icy wind blows through the trees. Fall is here, and school is out for the Thanksgiving holiday. At the local community center, a large group of teenagers has gathered. They are there to help cook and serve Thanksgiving dinner to people in need. The kids have been working hard setting the tables and helping in the kitchen. The wonderful smell of turkey and dressing fills the air. A few boys are cutting big slices of pumpkin pie. Some of the girls carry folding chairs to put around the long tables. The boys take pans of hot rolls out of the oven. Men and women from other service clubs have come to help. However, most of today's helpers are students from a nearby school. As the first visitors open the door, they can hear the sounds of workers chattering and pots and pans clanking. Soon everyone is sitting around the tables, enjoying the Thanksgiving dinner.

1. Why do you think these students came to help? Write what you think.

Extra help is needed around the holidays. However, people who want to help others are welcome any time of the year. Young people can make a big difference in their world. You might ask yourself, "What can one person do?" Here's the story of one girl who found a way to help others as she struggled to get over her own grief.

Name _____   Date _____

What One Girl Did

Angela, an eighth grader, was 9 years old when she started Project Smiles. Angela's inspiration was her baby brother, Daniel. Daniel became very sick and had to make many visits to the hospital. Angela often brought her brother some stuffed toys to make him laugh. She also noticed that other children in the hospital looked sad and lonely. So Angela decided to bring more stuffed animals for the other children. Angela and another brother pooled their own money to buy teddy bears. Angela tied paper hearts around the bears' necks. These paper hearts had the words "You're special" written on them. Then she gave these toys to the kids at the hospital.

Sadly, Angela's brother Daniel died at the age of 3 in 1997. Even though her inspiration was gone, her program, Project Smiles, lived on. By lifting the spirits of sick children, Angela was able to help herself deal with her great sadness.

Project Smiles has gotten a lot of attention from Angela's town and from around the country. She even received a letter from a person in New Zealand asking for help. She was so impressed by the letter that she sent one of her special teddy bears right away.

So far, Angela has given out about 3,000 stuffed toys to children. She also shares generously with adults who are living in nursing homes or shelters.

2. What kind of person is Angela? Tell why you think that.

Project Smiles started out small, but it has grown. Many people and businesses have given money and stuffed animals to the program.

In 1999, Angela received a Spirit of Community Award. She used the $1,000 award to buy a special computer for her brother Johnny. Johnny has a nerve disease, and he needs this computer to communicate with his family.

In April 2001, Angela was named a second-place winner in a magazine's Volunteerism Awards. These awards honored 6 girls and their extraordinary efforts to improve their communities. All of the winners met with First Lady Laura Bush. Angela also received a college scholarship and a check to give to her favorite project. She chose to donate the money to her local children's shelter.

Angela enjoys getting letters and cards from parents. These parents thank her for bringing stuffed animals to their children. However, she likes seeing the smiles on the children's faces even better. She hopes more people will want to help Project Smiles. Through Project Smiles, Angela's big heart has helped cheer up thousands of children and adults.

What You Can Do

You might be asking yourself, "What can I do to help?" There are many different ways for you to help people in need. First you should think about what you might like to do. Whom do you want to help? Do you love animals? Then maybe you can help out at an animal shelter. These shelters always need volunteers to help care for the animals and keep the cages clean. Maybe you would rather help your fellow students by tutoring someone who needs help in his or her classes. Those homework problems that you zipped through last night could be giving other kids fits! Have you noticed how some people seem lonely at school? You can be a friend to someone just by smiling and taking the time to get to know him or her.

3. Which of the tasks above do you think would be the most interesting? Tell why you think so.

There are organizations in your community that help people in need. The United Way might be a good place to find out how you can help. Smaller groups work with the United Way to find volunteers. Most churches and temples have programs to collect items such as canned goods and winter coats for people who need  them. You can help by donating clothes you don't wear anymore. You might also help collect food for a local food bank. Nursing homes need people to visit with their residents. You might bring a group of friends to sing to the residents, or maybe you can just bring a smile.

You can find ways to give your time or talents by looking in your phone book or on the Internet. When you help other people, you help yourself as well. You can learn about careers, understand different people, help solve problems, meet new friends, and even improve in school. Best of all, you let people know that teenagers are never too young to make a difference.

4. What would you like to do to help others?

Name _____ Date _____

Take a Stand—Wrap-Up

 Fill in the circle of the correct answer.

① This passage is mostly about—
   Ⓐ students who cook and serve Thanksgiving dinner.
   Ⓑ why Angela started a program called Project Smiles.
   Ⓒ how you can get involved in Project Smiles.
   Ⓓ ways young people can make a difference.

② The author writes about the Thanksgiving dinner in the first paragraph in order to—
   Ⓐ convince you to give food to people who need it.
   Ⓑ show an example of some young people who helped.
   Ⓒ describe a holiday special to people in the United States.
   Ⓓ tell a story about some students your age.

③ How might a children's hospital change after a visit from Project Smiles?
   Ⓐ The children would have teddy bears.
   Ⓑ The children would have free toothbrushes.
   Ⓒ The children would have letters written to them.
   Ⓓ The children would play games together.

④ What happened to Angela in 2001?
   Ⓐ Project Smiles began.   Ⓒ She made her first teddy bear.
   Ⓑ Her brother got sick.   Ⓓ She won a special award.

⑤ Why is volunteering a good thing to do? Give two examples from the passage.

_____

_____

⑥ How could you find a job helping people where you live? Use examples from the passage to tell how.

_____

_____

Name _____ Date _____

Unit 2

RESPECT ALL VOICES

To be respected, people need to respect others. All people deserve to have their thoughts and feelings considered. Think about how you show respect for others. Write about this in the boxes.

Respect

The people I live with:	Neighbors:
Teachers:	Friends:

Name _____ Date _____

Think about a time when you did not feel that you were respected. Describe what happened.

How did this make you feel?

How did it change the way you act toward other people?

GETTING READY TO READ

Name _____ Date _____

Strategy: Making Inferences, Drawing Conclusions

Sometimes when you read, you have to figure out what the author means. This is called *making inferences* or *drawing conclusions*. For example, if Justin has cookie crumbs around his mouth and the cookie jar is empty, you would draw the conclusion that Justin ate the cookies. When you read, story details and your own knowledge and experiences help you make inferences.

 Read the story below. Then make an inference or draw a conclusion about how Lisa feels at the end of the story.

> Lisa is a **part-time exterminator**. Yesterday she met a man who lives in a **duplex**. He was sitting in a **recliner** and breathing from an oxygen tank. She **delved** into the reason why he needed the tank. "I have **emphysema**," he said. "I worked in that chemical laboratory **complex** with the glass **facade**. I was exposed to poison." He pulled out a pen and his **checkbook** to pay Lisa. He handed her the pen. "I got this **trinket** when I retired," he said.
>
> Lisa began to sweat. The pen had the same design on it as the chemicals she used at work.

 Does Lisa start to sweat because the day is hot, or is there another reason? You have to make an inference.

Why does Lisa start to sweat? _____

How does she feel? _____

What makes her feel this way? _____

_____

Thinking about the meaning of information in a story will help you understand and enjoy what you read.

Name _____ Date _____

Vocabulary Builder

The words in the box come from the story you just read. You will see these words again in the story you are about to read.

 Complete each sentence with one of the words from the box. The first one has been done for you.

part-time
facade
delved
complex
trinket
duplex
emphysema
checkbook
recliner
exterminator

1) I am the word ___*part-time*___. If you don't work all the time but you do work some of it, then that is me.

2) I am the word _____. You can call me if you need to get rid of bugs or mice. I am someone you don't want to call twice.

3) I am the word _____. If you need to buy something but you don't have cash, maybe I can help.

4) I am the word _____. I am the front of a building, not the back.

5) I am the word _____. I am one building with two places to live inside.

6) I am the word _____. If you want to lie back and relax, I am the chair for you.

7) I am the word _____. When you dug or searched for something, that was me.

8) I am the word _____. I am a group of buildings.

9) I am the word _____. If your lungs are sick, then it might be me that you have.

10) I am the word _____. Something small or of little value might be me.

Purpose for Reading

Now you are going to read about a girl who is going through some hard times. Things seem to be getting worse. Read to find out what happens.

The Visit

When I left my **part-time** job at Ling's Newsstand, it was 8:05 P.M. It was an ordinary Thursday night. The air was cold, and I could see my breath in the air as I pushed my bike down the sidewalk. Nobody else was outside except Eddie.

Eddie has lived on the street as long as I can remember, and I'm 15 years old. I don't know how old he is. His skin is wrinkled, but his hair isn't gray.

"Hey, Eddie," I said. He sat against the brick **facade** of Quick 'N' Good Cleaners. He was wrapped up in his blanket.

---

part-time (PAHRT tym) *adjective* Part-time describes work or study that involves fewer hours than it would in a full schedule.

facade (fuh SAHD) *noun* A facade is the front of a building.

"Got something to eat, Rosa?" Eddie asked.

"Sure," I said. I **delved** into my jacket pocket and pulled out a bag. Inside the bag was a donut that Ms. Ling had given me for a snack.

I gave the bag to Eddie, and he tucked it into the pocket of his tattered jacket. "Thanks a lot. How was work?" Eddie inquired.

I shrugged and said, "The usual. Ms. Ling complained about how expensive things are to stock, and the customers complained about how expensive things are to buy."

"People complain, all right," Eddie said. "It seems like you, me, and most people around here are going through hard times."

> **1. What do you think Eddie means by "hard times"?**

"It sure does."

"Hey," Eddie said. "Did you hear about the office **complex** that Martin Developments is putting up on State Street? Maybe it'll bring a lot of money into our neighborhood."

"Maybe," I said. "But most of our homes are still in bad shape."

"Maybe this will help," Eddie said, holding out his hand. "Here's a **trinket** I found on the street this morning." He was holding a woman's watch with what looked like tiny diamonds around the face. "For you, because you're a good kid."

---

delved (DEHLVD) *verb* If you have delved into something, you have dug into it.
complex (KAHM plehks) *noun* A complex is a group of buildings that are linked together.
trinket (TRIHNG kiht) *noun* A trinket is a small toy or piece of jewelry that did not cost a lot of money.

Name _____ Date _____

"Wow, Eddie! Are you sure you wouldn't rather sell it?"

He nodded. "You deserve it, going to school and working to help your family. Besides, you're always giving me stuff to eat."

I thanked Eddie and strapped the watch around my wrist. It read "8:21." Eddie snuggled down into his blanket, and I knew that our conversation was over.

My home was at the end of the block. It was a **duplex** with wobbly front steps. We had no next-door neighbors. They had moved out because of the mouse problem.

> **2. How do you think Rosa feels about where she lives? Tell why you think that.**

When I unlocked our front door, my father was typing on his ancient computer. He works for local businesses, typing flyers. He has **emphysema**, a disease that makes it hard to breathe. Sometimes he has to breathe oxygen from a tank. Because of the emphysema, he doesn't get out much.

My 16-year-old sister, Teresa, was on the sofa with the **checkbook**. I dropped onto the **recliner**.

Teresa said, "We have almost enough money to pay all the bills. We'll hold off on some until Rosa and I get paid on the fifteenth."

---

duplex (DOO plehks) *noun* A duplex is a house that has been divided into two separate units.
emphysema (ehm fuh SEE muh) *noun* Emphysema is a disease that makes breathing difficult because the tissue in the lungs is damaged.
checkbook (CHEHK buk) *noun* A checkbook is a small book that has forms for writing checks and a place to record how much you spend.
recliner (rih KLY nuhr) *noun* A recliner is an armchair that you can adjust to lean back.

Dad turned and smiled at us. "I'm proud of you both," he said. "The neighbors tell me how much they admire you for working and going to school."

> **3. Do you think Rosa's job is important to her family? Tell why you think it is or is not.**

Just then, there was a knock on the door. It was our landlady, Marge Austin. She bounced in with a toss of her head.

"I'm sorry I'm late," she called. "I know you're having problems with your radiators."

She tested the radiators, downstairs and up. She declared that they really needed professional attention and that she'd have workers come by sometime soon.

She opened the door to leave, but I grabbed her arm. I was tired of her putting things off.

Name _____ Date _____

"It's getting cold at night. We need heat now!" I said. "And I saw four mice yesterday! You promised the **exterminator** would get them all!"

Marge Austin's smile vanished. "My apologies. I'll call them again, I promise."

"Thanks," Dad said, and the landlady left.

Then Dad said, "Rosa, try not to lose your temper like that. She's doing her best."

"I'm tired of mice and broken radiators," I said.

Dad nodded. "Yelling doesn't help. Things will get better soon, so try to be patient."

> **4. What kind of person do you think Rosa is? Explain your answer.**

Early the next morning, I awoke to a banging on the door. I stumbled downstairs and opened the door. Two police officers were standing on the porch.

"Rosa Gonzalez?" asked one.

I stared, and then said, "Yes?"

"A store in the neighborhood was robbed last night. We think you might know something about it."

---

exterminator (ehk STUR muh nayt uhr) *noun* An exterminator is someone you pay to get rid of mice, roaches, and other pests in your house.

Name _____ Date _____

Thinking About the Selection

 Fill in the circle of the correct answer.

1. What is this story mostly about?
   - Ⓐ Rosa's part-time job at Ling's Newsstand
   - Ⓑ Rosa's problems at home and work
   - Ⓒ Rosa's friends at school and work
   - Ⓓ Rosa's relationship with her sister

2. Who is Eddie?
   - Ⓐ Rosa's best friend from school
   - Ⓒ a man in Rosa's neighborhood
   - Ⓑ a person with whom Rosa works
   - Ⓓ Rosa's boss at work

3. What is the most important reason Rosa and her sister work?
   - Ⓐ They like what they do and think it is interesting.
   - Ⓑ They need the money to help support their family.
   - Ⓒ They want extra money to pay for clothes and music.
   - Ⓓ They want to be like their friends, who all have jobs.

4. Rosa is upset with Marge Austin because Ms. Austin—
   - Ⓐ should do more to help Rosa's family.
   - Ⓑ says she will not help Rosa's family.
   - Ⓒ will not hire Rosa's father for a job.
   - Ⓓ never comes to the duplex to see Rosa's family.

5. How does Rosa probably feel at the end of this story? Tell why you think so.

   _____

   _____

6. Describe Rosa's neighborhood, using details from the story.

   _____

   _____

WRITE ABOUT IT!

Name _____ Date _____

Prewriting

Speech Planner

In "The Visit," Rosa's family is having problems with money. Rosa is loyal to her job at Ling's Newsstand. She works hard and respects Ms. Ling. Think about something or someone you are dedicated to. This could be a job, a team, a cause, or a person you know. If you were giving a speech, how would you prove that you are dedicated?

 Fill in the chart below. Give three ways that you are dedicated to something or someone. Give examples.

Something/Someone I am dedicated to:
_____

What I would never do against this thing or person is:
_____

The first way I am dedicated is:

An example of this is:

The second way I am dedicated is:

An example of this is:

The third way I am dedicated is:

An example of this is:

Name _____ Date _____

A Plan for Writing

Something to Prove

A speech is spoken to a crowd. People often use speeches to prove something to others. A speech must include good examples in order to change people's thoughts.

 Write a speech that tries to prove that you are dedicated to something. Use the ideas from your chart.

Tell people why you are speaking.	Ladies and Gentlemen! I am here today to prove to you just how dedicated I am to _____. I would never _____.
Tell the first way you are dedicated.	One way I am dedicated is _____. An example of this is that _____ _____.
Tell the second way you are dedicated.	Another way I am dedicated is _____ _____. An example of this is that _____ _____.
Tell the final way you are dedicated.	The final way I am dedicated is _____ _____. An example of this is _____ _____.

Writing

 Write a speech to prove that you are dedicated to something or someone. Use the plan above to help you. Tell people the ways you are dedicated. Give good examples. You can add more details, but follow the order of your plan. Write your speech on a separate sheet of paper.

Name _____ Date _____

Strategy Workout: Fiction

Plot

The *plot* is what happens in a story. The events of a story usually revolve around some problem. At the end of the story, the problem is usually solved.

 Fill in the chart below to tell about the story you just read.

How this story started:

What happened next:

What I predict will happen later:

What I think the problem is:

www.harcourtschoolsupply.com
© Harcourt Achieve Inc. All rights reserved.

Unit 2: Why Me?
Reading Workout Book 4, SV 9781419099076

Name _____ Date _____

Words, Words, Words

Compound Words

Compound words are made of two smaller words. The author used compound words in the story you read. For example, the word *checkbook* is made of two smaller words.

check + book = checkbook

These smaller words help you know the meaning of the compound word. Look at the words *check* and *book*. They show that a checkbook is a book of checks.

 Read the words in the boxes. Then read the sentences below. Choose one word from box A and one from box B to make a compound word that fits in each sentence. Each word is used once.

A	B
land	time
part	stand
down	thing
some	stairs
some	lady
news	time

1. Rosa works at a _____ job.

2. She asks her _____ to fix all of the problems in her home.

3. Ms. Austin says she will make sure they are fixed _____.

4. The next morning, Rosa hears a knock and goes _____ to answer the door.

5. The police are at the door to tell her that the _____ was robbed last night.

6. They think Rosa might know _____ about it.

GETTING READY TO READ

Name _____ Date _____

Strategy: Making Inferences, Drawing Conclusions

When you make inferences or draw conclusions, you figure out information that is not written in the passage you are reading. You use details and your own experiences. If you are reading about a person, you might ask yourself if this person is like other people you know. You might think about how you would act or feel in this person's place. Thinking about yourself and others will help you draw conclusions as you read.

 Read the passage below. Think about making inferences and drawing conclusions while you read.

> I am a **prosecuting lawyer**. My job is to prove that the **accused** is guilty. My **clients** are the state and its people. I almost always get a guilty **verdict**.
>
> I am in the middle of a tough case that is being **tried** in front of a **jury**. I am sure the **defendant committed** the crime. However, I have only one piece of evidence. His **saliva** was at the crime scene. Will this be enough to persuade a jury to **convict** him?

 What conclusions can you make from this passage? Answer the questions below to tell what you think.

Do you think the lawyer will win this case?   *yes* / *no* (circle one)

Tell what makes you think so. _____

_____

_____

_____

_____

| **Thinking about more than just the words you read will make reading more interesting.** |

Name _____ Date _____

Vocabulary Builder

The words in the box come from the passage you just read. You will see these words again in the passage you are about to read.

➡ **Choose a word from the box to complete each sentence. Write the letters of the word on the blanks. The first word has been done for you. When you are finished, the letters in the circles will make a word. This word tells what might happen to someone who commits a crime.**

accused
clients
committed
convict
defendant
jury
prosecuting lawyer
saliva
~~tried~~
verdict

1. His case was t r(i)e d, and he was found innocent.
2. He was at work when the crime happened, so he could not have __ __ __(_)__ __ __ __ the crime.
3. A (_)__ __ __ __ __ __ __ __ __ __ __ __ __ __ __ __ __ __ tries to prove that the person charged with the crime is guilty.
4. If you serve on a __ __(_)__ , you might have to decide if a person is guilty or innocent.
5. The judge announced the __ __ __ __(_)__ __ : not guilty.
6. When she kissed the stolen jewel, she did not know the police could identify her from her (_)__ __ __ __ __.
7. There was so much evidence that it was not a hard decision to __(_)__ __ __ __ __ __ the criminal.
8. The __ __ __ __(_)__ __ __ __ told the court he was not guilty of the crime.
9. The lawyer had so many __ __ __(_)__ __ __ that he was always busy.
10. When the police charged the suspect with the crime, he became known as the __ __ __ __ __ __(_).

Answer: Someone who commits a crime might be __ __ __ __ __ __ __ __ __ __ __.

Name _____ Date _____

Purpose for Reading

Now you are going to read about a man who might have been wrongly sent to jail. Read to find out what happens.

The Crime Scene and Evidence

A murder victim is discovered. The police search the crime scene for tiny scraps of evidence. They piece them all together and arrest a suspect. Is the **accused** guilty of the crime?

---

1. Why do you think evidence is so important in police work?

In the early 1980s, Kenneth Waters was charged with a murder. His sister, Betty Anne Waters, was sure that Kenneth was innocent.

Kenneth was **tried** in a Massachusetts court. At the trial, the lawyer for the state attempted to prove that Kenneth was guilty. The lawyer for the state also is called the **prosecuting lawyer**.

---

accused (uh KYOOZD) *noun* The accused is the person who is charged with a crime.
tried (TRYD) *verb* Tried means "put on trial in a court of law."
prosecuting lawyer (PRAHS uh kyoot ihng LAW yuhr) *noun* The prosecuting lawyer is the lawyer who tries to prove a person is guilty of a crime.

The defense lawyer presented Kenneth's side of the story. He said that Kenneth had an alibi and couldn't have **committed** the murder. He had been somewhere else when the murder happened.

As Betty Anne sat in court and listened to the lawyers, so did the **jury**. The members of the jury listened carefully to all the evidence presented during the trial. Then they voted on whether Kenneth was guilty or not guilty. To **convict** Kenneth, members of the jury had to believe that he was guilty.

After they heard the evidence, the jury decided on a **verdict** of guilty. Betty Anne was horrified. She watched as her brother was taken away to spend the rest of his life in prison.

This trial was not Kenneth's last chance to show that he was not guilty. When a trial is over, the **defendant** can appeal a guilty verdict in an appeals court. This court hears the case again to decide whether the verdict should change or stay the same.

2. Why do you think the justice system has established an appeals court?

Kenneth appealed the verdict. Betty Anne was sure that he would be freed. She was wrong. The verdict didn't change.

---

committed (kuh MIHT ihd) *verb* Someone who committed a crime did something that was against the law.
jury (JUR ee) *noun* A jury is a group of people who make a decision in a court case.
convict (kuhn VIHKT) *verb* To convict means "to find someone guilty of a crime."
verdict (VUR dihkt) *noun* A verdict is the decision of guilty or not guilty in a court case.
defendant (dee FEHN duhnt) *noun* A defendant is a person against whom charges are filed.

Betty Anne was sure that her brother wasn't the killer. She didn't know how to help him, though. She was raising two children and couldn't afford to pay more lawyers.

A Do-It-Yourself Approach

Betty Anne decided that she would study to become a lawyer. Then she could fight to free her brother. It would be a difficult task because Betty Anne hadn't even finished high school. She had to go to school, work, and take care of her children.

First she finished high school. Then she took college classes. Betty Anne finally entered law school in 1995. By then, Kenneth already had served 12 years in prison.

In law school, Betty Anne learned about evidence. For hundreds of years, juries mostly heard accounts from witnesses and from officers who investigated crimes. More recently, police had begun using fingerprints as evidence. Each human being has fingerprints unlike those of any other person. Fingerprints can help show whether the accused was at the crime scene.

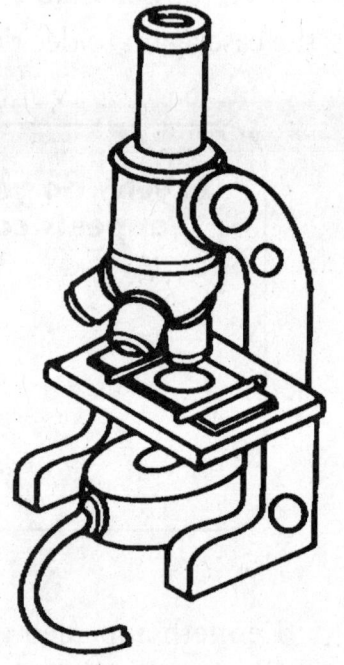

The newest kind of evidence interested Betty Anne most. This evidence was based on DNA, a chemical pattern that occurs in every cell of the body. A person's DNA is the same whether it is in hair, **saliva**, blood, tissue, or other body parts. Like fingerprints, no two people's DNA is exactly alike. Police sometimes find bits of hair, saliva, or blood at a crime scene. These clues can be very important.

---

saliva (suh LY vuh) *noun* Saliva, or spit, is a mixture of fluids in the mouth.

> **3. Why do you think Betty Anne was most interested in DNA evidence?**

No one had used DNA evidence in Kenneth's trial. Betty Anne wondered if this type of evidence might prove he was innocent.

What DNA Proved

In 1998, after Betty Anne became an attorney, she spent most of her time working on her brother's case. She took cases for some friends, but she had no other **clients**.

To help her brother, Betty Anne knew that she needed evidence from the crime scene. Did the evidence still exist? Massachusetts law said that evidence could be thrown away ten years after all appeals were completed. More than ten years had passed since Kenneth's appeals.

Betty Anne kept asking a courthouse worker to look for any evidence that still might be stored somewhere. Finally the worker found a box of evidence in the courthouse basement. The box held bloody items that had been found at the crime scene.

---

clients (KLY uhnts) *noun* Clients are a lawyer's customers.

A DNA test proved that Kenneth's blood didn't match the criminal's blood found at the crime scene. Betty Anne shared this information and other new evidence with a group of lawyers. This group of lawyers helped prisoners like Kenneth use new DNA evidence to challenge verdicts. After nearly twenty years in prison, Kenneth was freed.

4. Do you think Betty Anne continued to work as a lawyer? Tell why you think that.

Name _____   Date _____

Thinking About the Selection

 Fill in the circle of the correct answer.

1. This passage is mostly about how—
   - Ⓐ a jury is selected for a case.
   - Ⓑ a judge decides if a person is guilty.
   - Ⓒ one man who was wrongly jailed was freed.
   - Ⓓ DNA evidence was first used in U.S. courts.

2. U.S. courts have a system of appeals so that—
   - Ⓐ victims of crimes can make sure criminals stay in jail.
   - Ⓑ juries can have another chance to think about a case.
   - Ⓒ people convicted of crimes can have a second chance.
   - Ⓓ judges can disagree with juries if they want to.

3. How long did it take Betty Anne Waters to prove Kenneth's innocence?
   - Ⓐ one year
   - Ⓑ five years
   - Ⓒ ten years
   - Ⓓ twenty years

4. Betty Anne Waters helped her brother by becoming a—
   - Ⓐ police officer.
   - Ⓑ lawyer.
   - Ⓒ detective.
   - Ⓓ judge.

5. How did Kenneth Waters's sister finally prove that he was innocent?
   _____
   _____

6. What problem with the court system does Kenneth Waters's case show?
   _____
   _____

WRITE ABOUT IT!

Prewriting

Idea Chart

In "The Crime Scene and Evidence," Betty Anne Waters worked hard to prove her brother's innocence. Think about someone you know who has been unfairly treated or blamed for something he or she did not do. How would you show that the person deserved more respect?

 Fill in the chart below. Tell about the person who has been treated badly. Tell why that person should be helped.

Someone Who Has Been Treated Unfairly

The Unfair Treatment or Problem

Three Reasons Why This Person Should Be Treated Better

1.

2.

3.

Filling out this page will help you organize your ideas before you start writing.

Name _____ Date _____

A Plan for Writing

This Is Unfair

A persuasive essay tells an opinion. It tries to get people to think or feel the same way the writer does. A persuasive essay must give good reasons, or else people might not change their minds. The best reason appears last so that people will remember it.

 Write a persuasive essay to tell about someone who has been treated unfairly. Make people realize why this person should be treated better. Use ideas from your chart.

Tell about the unfairness.	Someone who has been treated unfairly is _____. The way that this person has been treated badly is _____.
Tell the first reason more respect is needed.	This person deserves more respect because _____.
Tell the second reason more respect is needed.	The second reason this person should be treated better is _____.
Tell the final reason more respect is needed.	Most importantly, this person should be treated better because _____.

Writing

 Write a persuasive essay to help someone be treated better. Use the plan above to help you. Give three good reasons why the person deserves more respect. You can add more details, but follow the order of your plan. Write your persuasive essay on a separate sheet of paper.

Name _____ Date _____

Strategy Workout: Nonfiction

Headers

Books and selections that have a lot of information are often separated into sections. Chapters are big sections of information. Within chapters, there might be sections that have different titles. These titles are called *headers*.

Headers are like chapter titles, only they tell you what you can expect to find in a certain section of a chapter or article. Headers are often printed in *italics* or in **bold** print so that you can see them easily. Headers help readers find and organize information as they read.

To remember what you read, it can be useful to take notes about each section.

 The selection you just read had three sections. Each section was introduced with a passage title or header. Write the titles at the top of each column. Then find three ideas you think are the most important in each section. Write them below the titles.

Passage Title: _____	First Section Header: _____	Second Section Header: _____
1.	4.	7.
2.	5.	8.
3.	6.	9.

 The title of each section gives the reader an idea about what was included in that part of the selection. What other titles would have done the same thing? Write your ideas below.

10. Another good title for this passage would be: _____

11. Another good header for the first section would be: _____

12. Another good header for the second section would be: _____

Name _____ Date _____

Words, Words, Words

Reference Materials: Encyclopedias

Encyclopedias are kept in the reference section of the library. An encyclopedia has some information on almost every topic.

Encyclopedias are organized by the alphabet in different **volumes**, or books. The first volume includes topics that start with the letter *A*. The last volume is usually an **index**. You can use this to look up the pages for different topics.

The top of each page lists **guide words**, just like in a dictionary. Each topic starts with an **entry word**.

 Use the words in the box to fill in the blanks in the sentences.

After reading this passage, I wanted to know more about criminal justice in the United States. I looked up the words *criminal justice* in the encyclopedia.

The (**1.**) _____ told me that I would find the information in C: 268. I looked in (**2.**) _____ 2, on page 268. I saw the (**3.**) _____ *Crete* and *Croatia* at the top of the page. Then I found the (**4.**) _____ I was looking for.

| entry words |
| guide words |
| index |
| volume |

 Think of another topic about which you would like to know more. Answer the questions below.

5. What topic do you want to know more about? _____

6. What entry word could you use to look in an encyclopedia? _____

7. What guide words might be on that page? _____

8. What other entry words might have information about your topic? _____

GETTING READY TO READ

Strategy: Recognizing Author's Viewpoint, Purpose

An author's reason for writing is called the *author's purpose*. Authors might write to entertain, to inform, to give directions or instructions, or to persuade the reader to think a certain way. When you read, think about the author's purpose. This will help you think carefully about what you've read.

 Read the passage below. Think about the author's purpose for writing.

> A **co-worker** told me about a difficult race in which you swim, bike, and run. I **feigned** interest, but I was sure I'd do well because I'm a **top-notch** swimmer. I decided to compete in the race.
>
> Hundreds of other swimmers **jostled** and **splattered** me. The swim event **waterlogged** my **eardrums**. **Grimacing** through the swim, I quit. I couldn't **fathom** how others went on to bike and run. I **blubbered** loudly as I went home and admitted I was wrong.

 Place a check ✓ by the choice that you think best describes the author's purpose for writing this passage. Then describe what made you think that was the author's purpose.

The author's purpose for writing was to:
- ☐ explain how to train for a race.
- ☐ convince you that a race is difficult.
- ☐ share an entertaining story.

I think this was the author's purpose for writing because

_____

_____

Remember that an author might have more than one reason for writing. This author wanted to tell about her experience so that anyone thinking about trying such a race would know how difficult it would be. This author also probably wanted to write in a funny way so that readers would pay more attention to the message.

> **Thinking about the author's purpose will help you understand and remember what you read.**

Name _____ Date _____

Vocabulary Builder

The words in the box come from the passage you just read. You will see these words again in the story you are about to read.

 Write the correct word in each sentence. This will help you learn about the words before you begin reading. The first one has been done for you.

co-worker
eardrums
waterlogged
fathom
grimacing
top-notch
feigned
blubbered
splattered
jostled

1. Work is more fun if you get along with every _co-worker_.

2. He cried and _____ so loudly that I knew that something was really wrong.

3. Your _____ are the parts of your ears that separate the insides of your ears from the outside.

4. I did such an excellent job on my paper that my teacher said I was a _____ writer.

5. An hour's worth of pounding rain _____ us.

6. When he said he could not _____ the idea, he meant that he could not understand it thoroughly.

7. Her _____ face showed that she was in pain.

8. The crowd _____ him into the train.

9. She was not interested even though she _____ excitement.

10. When my dog shook herself off, she _____ me with mud.

Purpose for Reading

Now you are going to read a story. Four teens and two counselors are heading off to Gull Island for a survival camp program. Read to find out about some of the lessons they learn.

How Coyote Learned the River Code

April 18

What a day! I was standing on the deck of the ferry when the clouds came in dark and thick. My **co-worker**, Julia, and I were in charge of 4 mischievous teens from the Neighborhood Club for Boys and Girls. We were on our way to the Survival Program on Gull Island. There were 6 counselors and 12 kids in the program, and we were stuck together for 5 days.

Don't get me wrong. Our four teens aren't bad, just a bunch of goof-offs. Jack nearly popped my **eardrums** with his constant noise. Pedro picked a fight with Liz, which was not very bright since she's the tallest and strongest teen in the group.

> **1. How does the narrator feel about his job? Tell why you think that.**

May fooled me with her innocent baby face at first, but when she thought I wasn't looking, I caught her throwing potato chips to the seals in the harbor.

---

co-worker (KOH wurk uhr) *noun* A co-worker is someone who works with another person, usually in the same kind of job.

eardrums (IHR druhmz) *noun* Eardrums are thin pieces of tissue in the ears that move back and forth when sound waves hit them.

The good news is that Julia won't put up with any nonsense. I learned that much this afternoon. Right after Gull Island came into view, the skies opened up, and buckets of rain **waterlogged** us. The group raced inside from the deck of the ferry and sat down on some benches around a table. Everybody was dripping wet. Jack shouted, "My CD player got soaked!"

Julia gave him a look and said, "Remember the camp rules that you all agreed to follow? Number three: *No CD players, tape players, or radios are allowed at the Survival Program.* Hand it over, Jack."

"Oh, you've got to be kidding," Jack wailed.

waterlogged (WAWT uhr lawgd) *verb* Waterlogged means "soaked or filled with water."

Julia put out her hand for the CD player, but Jack crossed his arms and tried to stare her down. He had no luck. Finally he sighed loudly and surrendered the CD player.

"Hey, Danso, does that mean there's no TV on Gull Island?" Liz asked me, as if she couldn't **fathom** such a possibility.

> **2. Why do you think the four neighborhood kids are going to the camp on Gull Island?**
>
>

"That's right, no TV," I said. "Listen up—I want you all to have a great time, but you've got to respect the rules."

"Forget the rules. I'm soaked," Pedro said, **grimacing**.

Then Julia said, "That reminds me of a story. Since we're the entertainment around here, I'll tell you about the time of the first rainstorm."

"Who cares?" Pedro asked.

Julia ignored him and told this story, which got everybody's mind off TVs and rain for a while.

---

fathom (FATH uhm) *verb* To fathom something is to understand it.
grimacing (GRIH mihs ihng) *adjective* Grimacing means "making an unhappy face."

Coyote lived near a river and loved to eat fish, but he hated fishing.

Now, every animal that lived by the river knew the River Code: *Don't mess with another creature's fish.*

Coyote knew the River Code, but he didn't care. He knew that Bear was a **top-notch** fisher and that Bear loved to nap. More than once, Coyote had waited until Bear fell asleep, and then he had stolen Bear's fishing bag.

> **3. What do you think is going to happen to Coyote?**

One day Bear got his revenge. He went out and found a bear trap. He slipped the trap into his fishing bag as a surprise for Coyote.

Later that afternoon, Bear **feigned** sleep, and sure enough, Coyote raced off with the fishing bag, bear trap and all. Bear followed him secretly. When Coyote reached his home on the mountaintop, he opened the bag, put in his paw, and—"AHHHHH!" he cried. The trap had clamped down on his paw.

Coyote **blubbered** so hard that Bear finally took pity on him. Bear came out of hiding and said, "I hope you learned your lesson." He opened the trap for Coyote. "From now on, follow the River Code."

---

top-notch (TAHP nahch) *adjective* Top-notch means "excellent."
feigned (FAYND) *verb* Feigned means "pretended."
blubbered (BLUHB uhrd) *verb* Blubbered means "cried loudly."

Name _____ Date _____

4. Why do you think Julia is telling this story about Coyote and Bear?

Coyote nodded, but his paw hurt so much that he cried all night. His tears **splattered** onto the land below the mountain and caused the first rainstorm ever. From that day on, Coyote always remembered to respect the rules.

Just as Julia finished the story, our ferry docked at Gull Island. May must have **jostled** her bags, because a radio started blaring from her backpack. I didn't have to say a word. I just looked at her and waited. "OK, I get the point," she said, handing over the radio.

It's going to be an interesting five days.

---

splattered (SPLAT uhrd) *verb* Splattered means "splashed with drops of water or other liquid."
jostled (JAHS uhld) *verb* Jostled means "bumped."

Name _____ Date _____

Thinking About the Selection

 Fill in the circle of the correct answer.

1. This story is mostly about—
   Ⓐ what caused the first rainstorm ever.
   Ⓑ why Bear and Coyote do not get along.
   Ⓒ how four kids learned about following rules.
   Ⓓ why radios or CD and tape players are not allowed at camp.

2. Who is telling the story about the trip to Gull Island?
   Ⓐ a counselor named Julia
   Ⓑ a counselor named Danso
   Ⓒ a camper named Pedro
   Ⓓ a camper named Liz

3. Coyote gets into trouble when he—
   Ⓐ cries and gets the other animals wet.
   Ⓑ blubbers so loudly he wakes up Bear.
   Ⓒ takes another animal's fish.
   Ⓓ sets a trap for Bear.

4. The lesson of the story about Bear and Coyote is best described as—
   Ⓐ *work is more important than fun.*
   Ⓑ *it is important to respect the rules.*
   Ⓒ *you can't always get along with everyone.*
   Ⓓ *how you act is more important than what you say.*

5. Does Danso like being a counselor? Use details from the story to tell why you think he does or does not.

   _____
   _____

6. Why does Julia tell a story instead of just telling the kids what lesson she wants them to learn?

   _____
   _____
   _____

WRITE ABOUT IT!

Prewriting

Name _____ Date _____

Idea Chart

In "How Coyote Learned the River Code," Jack has to hand his CD player over to Julia because the rules say he cannot bring it to the island. Many people enjoy music and would have a hard time living without it. Think about some music that you have heard. It could be a kind of music, a performer, a song on the radio, or a CD.

 Fill in the chart below. Give two reasons why you like the music and two reasons why you do not like it. Then tell whether you think other people would like it.

Music: _____

Some details about this: _____
_____

What I Like About This Music	What I Don't Like About This Music
1. _____	1. _____
2. _____	2. _____

Would I tell someone to try listening to this music?   *yes / no* (circle one)

Name _____ Date _____

 A Plan for Writing

Music Review

A review tells people what is good and bad about something. It helps people decide if something is worth their money or time.

➡ **Write a music review. Tell if you think someone else would like the music. Use ideas from your chart.**

Describe what you are reviewing.	This is a review of _____.
	This is _____.
Tell what you like about the music.	I like this music because _____
	_____.
	Also _____
	_____.
Tell what you don't like about the music.	I don't like this music because _____
	_____.
	Also _____
	_____.
Tell if someone else should buy it.	I think that most people *would / would not* (circle one) like this music. I suggest that other people *should / should not* (circle one) hear it because _____
	_____.

 Writing

➡ Write a music review on a separate sheet of paper. Use the plan above to help you. Describe what you like and what you do not like about the music. Then tell whether you think others would like it

Name _____ Date _____

Strategy Workout: Fiction

Theme

A *theme* is the message of a story. Authors often write stories to give a message to the reader. The reader enjoys reading the story and learns a lesson, too.

The story you just read told a story within a longer story. Both the longer story and the story within it had a message for the reader. Think about what message or lesson you could learn from these stories.

 Use what you know about themes to answer these questions.

1. What is the theme of the story of the campers going to Gull Island?

   _____
   _____

2. What in the story makes you think so?

   _____
   _____
   _____

3. What is the theme of the story of Coyote and the River Code?

   _____
   _____

4. What in that story makes you think so?

   _____
   _____
   _____

Words, Words, Words

Understanding Words with More Than One Meaning

Some words have more than one meaning. In the story you read, there were some words like this. For example, the word *point* has more than one meaning.

Point can mean: (**a**) a sharp tip or end (**b**) an important idea or message

 Read the sentences below. Then circle the letter for the meaning for the word *point* that goes with each sentence.

1. May got the *point* when Danso stared at her.   a.   b.

2. I sharpened my pencil until it had a good *point*.   a.   b.

 The underlined words from the story have more than one meaning. The meanings are written in the box. For each sentence, write the letter of the meaning for the word that fits in that sentence.

3. We were in charge of four kids. _____

4. All animals must follow the River Code. _____

5. Don't mess with another creature's fish. _____

6. He slipped the trap into his bag. _____

> charge (**a**) a responsibility or duty (**b**) to ask for payment
> code (**a**) a secret way of writing (**b**) a rule or law
> mess (**a**) a dirty or sloppy state (**b**) to touch or disturb
> slipped (**a**) put or moved secretly (**b**) slid by accident on a smooth surface

 Now write your own sentence with one of the words. Use a different meaning for *charge*, *code*, *mess*, or *slipped* than is used above.

_____

GETTING READY TO READ

Name _____ Date _____

Strategy: Recognizing Author's Viewpoint, Purpose

Authors have different viewpoints, or ideas. If an author wants to teach the reader how to do something, then the author probably thinks this thing is important. If an author writes to get the reader to think about something in a different way, this is probably the way the author thinks.

 As you read the passage below, think about the author's viewpoint.

> Joe lives in the **urban** neighborhood where I have **resided** for a year. My friend Max thinks Joe is from another planet. Joe is thin, and he has pointy ears and a huge head. Joe is so thin that Max says **starvation** must be common on Joe's planet. Joe can jump high, too. Max says **mystifying phenomena** like gravity must not affect him.
>
> Max isn't always **trustworthy**, so I **weighed** his arguments. We finally reached a **compromise**. I would talk to Joe and then report back to Max. "I hope Joe won't have **abducted** you," Max said. I'm not worried. Joe isn't really an alien with **humanoid** features. I'm sure he's just a human kid.

 Place a check ✓ by the choice that you think best describes this author's viewpoint. Then describe what made you think this was the author's viewpoint.

The author's viewpoint is that:

☐ Max might not always know what is right or true.
☐ Joe probably is not an alien from another planet.
☐ Max is probably right about Joe.
☐ Joe is probably an alien from another planet.

I think this is the author's viewpoint because _____
_____

Remember that sometimes you have to guess what the author thinks by what the author chooses to write about and the words the author uses.

Thinking about the author's viewpoint will help you be a more thoughtful reader.

Name _____ Date _____

Vocabulary Builder

The words in the box come from the passage you just read. You will see these words again in the passage you are about to read.

➡ **Complete each sentence with one of the words. The first one has been done for you.**

abducted
compromise
humanoid
mystifying
phenomena
resided
~~starvation~~
trustworthy
urban
weighed

1. I am the word ___starvation___. If you suffer from me, you need to eat.

2. I am the word _____. I describe something that isn't quite human.

3. I am the word _____. *Captured* and *kidnapped* are other words for me.

4. I am the word _____. I have to do with the city, not the country.

5. I am the word _____. I can mean what you did when you stepped on a scale or what you did when you considered two sides of a tale.

6. I am the word _____. I'm what you do when you settle your differences by giving up something.

7. I am the word _____. Other words that mean the same thing as me are *mysterious* or *confusing*.

8. I am the word _____. I start with the letters *ph*, but they sound like an *f*. I am events or things we observe in the world around us.

9. I am the word _____. I'm what you did when you lived in a place.

10. I am the word _____. You can rely on me.

Purpose for Reading

Now you are going to read about myths. People have always told stories to explain things that they did not know or understand. We still do. Read on and think about why we tell stories.

Old Myths and Modern Monsters

One day when Earth was still young, something happened that almost ended the human race. While a girl named Persephone picked flowers in a field, danger lurked nearby. A king from a distant kingdom was watching the girl and fell in love with her. He **abducted** Persephone and took her to his kingdom.

The girl's mother, Demeter, had power over all the plants on Earth. When she learned that her daughter had been kidnapped, she threatened to destroy all of Earth's fruits and vegetables. The human race would die of **starvation** if Persephone were not returned to her.

> **1. What evidence tells you this is not a true story?**

The most powerful being in this ancient world was Zeus. Zeus said he could free Persephone if she hadn't eaten any food in this other kingdom. Unfortunately, the girl had already tasted a bit of fruit.

abducted (ab DUHKT ehd) *verb* Abducted is to have captured or kidnapped someone.
starvation (stahr VAY shuhn) *noun* Starvation means "death from lack of food."

Name _____ Date _____

Zeus could not free her, but he reached a **compromise** with the king. Persephone could come home for part of every year, but she had to live with the king for the rest of the year. Still angry, Demeter allowed crops to grow only while her daughter was at home. The rest of the year, all of Earth's plants produced no food.

Ancient Myths

Does this sound like an entertaining story? Ancient Greeks told tales such as this one for a different reason. Their stories explained what they saw in the world around them. The story about Demeter's daughter helped people understand the changing seasons. When Persephone **resided** with the king, nothing grew. When she came back home, plants burst into life.

Many tales in the ancient world explained natural **phenomena**. One tale explained the daily cycle of the sun and moon. In this story, Apollo and Artemis rode chariots that pulled the sun and moon across the sky. Another story told about a woman named Pandora whose curiosity tempted her to open a special box. When she did, she accidentally let evil and disease into the world.

For centuries, people believed these tales. The old tales are now called *myths*. Myths are stories that explain natural events, history, or special qualities in people.

> **2. Do you think myths are mostly based on facts or opinions? Tell why you think that.**

---

compromise (KAHM pruh myz) *noun* A compromise is a way of reaching an agreement in which each side gives something up.
resided (rih ZYD ehd) *verb* Resided means "lived in a certain place."
phenomena (fuh NAHM uh nuh) *noun* Phenomena are events or conditions that we can observe in the world around us.

Today's Myths

You might think we no longer need myths. After all, scientists now offer other explanations for the seasons, the movements of the sun and moon, and disease. Yet we are still creating new myths. Why? We use myths to help us explain the unknown and predict the future. As a society, we use myths to guide behavior. What kinds of myths do we create?

Monster Tales

Imagine camping in the mountains and seeing a large, **humanoid** creature among the trees. It looks like a person but not exactly. You call it a monster. If you tell other people about it, they might look for the creature. They might even spot it or think they spot it. Soon everyone might be talking about the monster in the mountains.

UFO Sightings

A **mystifying** light darts across the sky. Could it be a spaceship from another planet? If no one gives you a better explanation, you might believe it is. Then a man on television claims he was taken to another planet. He describes it in such detail that you feel as if you were there.

---

humanoid (HYOO muh noyd) *adjective* Humanoid is having a human-like form or features.
mystifying (MIHS tuh fy ihng) *adjective* Mystifying means "confusing or mysterious."

3. Why might people believe stories about spaceships from another planet?

Superstitions

A superstition is a belief that an event or an action can influence future events. Imagine finding an unusual button on the street and putting it in your pocket. If the day went really well, you might tell friends that the button brought you good luck. Your friends might start looking for lucky buttons, too. You've created a superstition!

Urban Legends

A friend tells you a really scary story. You're not sure it's true, but your friend insists it happened to a **trustworthy** friend of a friend. It must be true! Plus, it's a good story, so you tell other people. You've just helped pass on an **urban** legend.

---

trustworthy (TRUHST wur thee) *adjective* A trustworthy person is someone who can be trusted.
urban (UR buhn) *adjective* Urban is having to do with a city or city life.

How Do We Know?

People tell each other many stories and insist that they're true. How can you tell if they are true or not? The best way to decide is to listen to arguments for both sides of the story. Some explanations might sound silly at first, but try listening anyway. Once you've **weighed** both sides, you can decide on your own explanation.

4. Why do you think the author wrote this paragraph?

weighed (WAYD) *verb* To have weighed something is to have considered it.

Name _____ Date _____

Thinking About the Selection

 Fill in the circle of the correct answer.

1. This passage is mostly about—
   - Ⓐ how to decide if a story you heard is true.
   - Ⓑ the myths of ancient Greek culture.
   - Ⓒ stories people tell to explain things.
   - Ⓓ reports of people seeing monsters or UFOs.

2. The myth at the beginning of this passage explains why—
   - Ⓐ Earth has different seasons.
   - Ⓑ people need food to live.
   - Ⓒ we have thunder and lightning.
   - Ⓓ people fall in love.

3. The author's reason for telling the myth at the beginning of this passage was to—
   - Ⓐ explain a situation you might not understand.
   - Ⓑ introduce the characters she would write about.
   - Ⓒ show one kind of modern urban legend.
   - Ⓓ give an example of one ancient myth.

4. Which is an example of a superstition?
   - Ⓐ a black cat bringing bad luck
   - Ⓑ a story about the Abominable Snowman
   - Ⓒ the Greek myth about King Midas and the golden touch
   - Ⓓ a sighting of a spaceship from another planet

5. What do you think this author's viewpoint is about myths? Does the author think they are important or not? Explain what makes you think so.

   _____
   _____

6. Compare and contrast ancient myths and the myths we tell today. Tell one way they are alike. Tell one way they are different.

   _____
   _____

WRITE ABOUT IT!

Prewriting

Name _____ Date _____

Idea Web

In "Old Myths and Modern Monsters," you learn that people create myths to explain things in nature or history. Think of something in the world that many people do not understand or that people did not understand at one time. What kind of story could explain it?

 Fill in the web below. Write down ideas for a myth. The myth could take place today or at another time.

Something Unexplained

How a Myth Could Explain This

What Happens in the Myth

1.

2.

3.

Filling out this page will help you organize your ideas before you start writing.

Name _____ Date _____

A Plan for Writing

Making Myths

A narrative tells a story. A myth is a kind of narrative that explains something mysterious or unknown. Myths are usually exciting so that people remember them.

 Write a new myth to explain something that is unknown or was unknown at one time. Use ideas from your web.

Tell about the thing to be explained.	Some people do not understand _____. This myth explains this. It is about _____ _____.
Tell what happened first.	Here is what happened. _____ _____ _____.
Tell what happened next.	Then _____ _____ _____.
Tell what happened last.	Finally _____ _____ _____. And that is how _____.

Writing

 Write a myth to explain something mysterious. Use the plan above to help you. Tell what the myth explains. Tell how it explains the unknown. You can add more details, but follow the order of your plan. Write your myth on a separate sheet of paper.

Name _____ Date _____

Strategy Workout: Nonfiction

Table of Contents and Index

A book's table of contents and index help readers find information quickly. The table of contents is in the front of a book. It tells the title of each chapter in the book. It also tells on what page each chapter starts. The index is in the back of the book. It lists people, places, and things in alphabetical order. The index tells which pages have information on these people, places, and things.

 Read the table of contents and index. Then answer the questions.

Contents

Chapter 1: Old Myths and
    Modern Monsters............... 1
Chapter 2: Things That Go
    Bump in the Night............. 8
Chapter 3: Are We Alone?.......... 21
Chapter 4: This Really Works!....... 33
Chapter 5: A Friend of a
    Friend Told Me............... 39
Chapter 6: I Want to Believe......... 52
Glossary.......................... 56
Index............................ 60

Use the table of contents and index when you need to find specific information in a book quickly.

Index

Greek myths 3
Superstitions 5, 33–38
Urban legends 6, 39–45
Zeus 2

 Use the table of contents and index to answer these questions.

1. How many chapters are in this book? _____

2. What is the title of the first chapter? _____

3. Which chapter probably tells about superstitions? _____

4. Which chapter probably tells about urban legends? _____

5. Which chapter probably tells tales about monsters? _____

6. Which chapter probably tells about UFO sightings? _____

7. Which pages tell about superstitions? _____

Name _____ Date _____

Words, Words, Words

Prefixes and Suffixes

A prefix is a set of letters that can be added to the beginning of some words. A suffix is a set of letters that can be added to the end of some words. Prefixes and suffixes change the meanings of words. For example, the word *prefix* has a prefix in itself. This prefix is the letters *pre-*.

 Read the sentences in the box. See how the underlined words change when a prefix or suffix is added. The prefix *pre-* means "before." The suffix *-ness* means "the state of being a certain way."

Before I started <u>school</u>, I went to **preschool**.

Jim is a <u>great</u> man and his actions showed his **greatness**.

 Read the following sentences. Then write what you think each prefix means.

1. The events and things we can explain and understand are **known**. Myths help us explain those things that are **unknown**.

   The prefix *un-* means _____.

2. If you know an interesting story, you probably will not just **tell** it once. You will probably **retell** it again and again.

   The prefix *re-* means _____.

 Read the following sentences. Then write down what you think each suffix means.

3. If you lie in bed thinking about monsters when you want to **sleep**, you may find that you have a **sleepless** night.

   The suffix *-less* means _____.

4. Zeus had the **power** to rescue Persephone because he was the most **powerful** being in the ancient world.

   The suffix *-ful* means _____.

Respect All Voices—Wrap-Up

What Does the Truth Have to Do with It?

Eric waited for the bus. Today was his first day at the new school, and he wasn't happy. When the bus came, he got on, sat down, and stared out the window.

> **1. Why do you think Eric is not happy? Write what you think.**

"Hi," a voice said. Eric turned and saw a girl leaning on the back of his seat. "My name's Angela," she continued. "Who are you? Are you new?"

"I'm Eric," he answered. "We just moved here from California."

"California—cool! OK, I have to ask. Do you have a **surfboard**?" Angela asked.

"No, I don't surf. Too many sharks," Eric answered.

"Oh! That sounds like a good reason to me," she said. "Do you have any pets?"

"I have a collie named Sheba. She's the best," he said. "What about you?"

"I have two crazy cats," Angela answered. She held out her right hand. "This scratch is from Tippy, and this big one is from Raven."

"Check this out," Eric said as he rolled up his left sleeve. A long, pinkish scar ran up the back of his arm. "I got this from tripping into a fence one time when I was playing with Sheba."

"Ouch!" Angela wrinkled her nose, and Eric smiled.

Soon the bus pulled up to the school, and everyone jumped out.

A few days later, Eric stood in the cafeteria line. He had been at this school for a week now, and Angela was the only person who had talked to him. He missed his old life.

Just then, several boys got in line behind Eric. He recognized the blond guy from his English class.

"Hey, aren't you the new kid from California?" the blond boy asked.

"Yeah. I'm Eric."

"I'm Brent."

Another boy, Trey, leaned around Brent's shoulder.

"Did you surf a lot there?" Trey asked, his eyes wide.

"Hey, have you ever been to a Lakers game?" Brent asked before Eric could answer.

2. Do you think Eric will make friends with Trey and Brent?

"Well, no, not really," Eric said. The boys' faces fell. Then Brent and Trey turned back toward their friends in line.

Eric couldn't believe it. This was the one chance he'd had all week to make some friends, and he had blown it! He hated being the new kid.

For the next few days, Eric waited for the bus after school and watched Brent and Trey playing basketball on the court past the parking lot. While they were having a great time, he had to get on the hot, boring bus to go home.

Then he remembered that day in the cafeteria line. He could have told Trey, "Sure, I've surfed." It was true. He had surfed—one time. Why couldn't he have bent the truth a tiny bit?

The next afternoon, Eric caught up to Brent and Trey and tried to seem casual.

"Hey, guys," he said.

"What's up, Eric?" Brent said.

"Remember when I said I didn't really surf?"

"Yeah, what about it?" Trey asked.

"Well, I meant that I haven't surfed a lot, but I did hit the waves sometimes," Eric said.

"Oh yeah?" Brent asked doubtfully. "What's it like?"

"Well, if you go out in the morning, the water's freezing. If you see the waves breaking about twenty feet out, you know they'll be good."

Eric told them surfing stories he'd heard from his friends back home. He wasn't sure if the stories were completely true, but Brent and Trey wouldn't know any better.

As the days passed, Eric told more stories about his surfing experiences. Later, he added the names of some movie stars he had seen in Los Angeles. He had never actually seen any, but saying that he had made Brent and Trey think he was cool.

One day, he claimed to have a basketball signed by Shaquille O'Neal. Brent's eyes had sparkled. "Shaquille O'Neal is my favorite player," he had said excitedly. Suddenly, Eric started worrying. What if Brent wanted to see the ball? What would Eric do then?

---

3. What do you think Eric will do next?

The other thing he had to worry about was Angela. He had already told her that he didn't surf. If she heard him talking to the guys, she would know that he was lying. He had to avoid her, at least for now.

Then one Friday it happened. Eric was standing by the bus with his friends, explaining how to wax a surfboard.

"Then you coat the bottom of the board with this thick goo—"

He didn't hear Angela walk up behind him.

"Hi, guys!" she said.

Eric almost jumped out of his skin. "Angela, what are you doing here?"

"I was wondering if you were riding the bus home today," Angela said. "What were you saying about a surfboard?"

"Oh, uh, I was just telling Trey and Brent how to wax one," he said.

"Really?" Angela looked confused. "I thought you said you didn't surf," she said.

"He does so surf," Trey said to Angela. "He even has a scar to prove it. Show her, Eric!"

Eric reluctantly rolled up his left sleeve.

"That?" Angela pointed at Eric's scar as she got on the bus. Just as the door was about to close, she called, "He got that from playing with his dog!"

Now Trey looked confused.

"So you just made up the surfing stuff?" he asked Eric.

"Well, yeah, but—" Eric stumbled over the words.

"What about the Lakers?" Brent asked, crossing his arms.

Eric glanced down. "No, I've never seen them play. But I almost did."

"And the autographed basketball?" Trey asked.

Eric just shook his head. This was it. He was going to lose his new friends.

"I knew it!" Brent laughed. "Didn't I tell you, Trey?"

4. How would you have felt if you were Brent or Trey?

"You knew?" Eric was shocked.

"Sure," Trey answered. "It was pretty obvious that day you just happened to mention surfing and the Lakers—a few days after we had talked about it at lunch."

"Really? I thought I was being smooth," Eric said. He felt his cheeks burning. All that worry and they knew he had been lying all along.

"I'm sorry about lying to you—I really am. I just thought you might like me more if I had cool things to talk about."

"We like you because you tell great stories, Eric. You don't have to say they're about you," Brent said.

Eric let out a big breath. It had been hard work pretending to be someone he wasn't.

"Wait until you hear the one my dad told me about the earthquake," he said as the three of them walked toward the basketball court.

Name _____ Date _____

Respect All Voices—Wrap-Up

 Fill in the circle of the correct answer.

1. This story is mostly about—
   - Ⓐ a boy who learns to make friends at a new school.
   - Ⓑ why surfboarding and basketball are so much fun.
   - Ⓒ the differences between boys and girls.
   - Ⓓ a boy and his pet dog, Sheba.

2. How does Eric feel at the beginning of the story?
   - Ⓐ bored
   - Ⓑ proud
   - Ⓒ glad
   - Ⓓ unhappy

3. What happens first in this story?
   - Ⓐ Eric meets Angela.
   - Ⓑ Eric waits for the bus.
   - Ⓒ Eric meets Brent and Trey.
   - Ⓓ Eric tells stories about surfing.

4. In this story, the word *surfboard* means—
   - Ⓐ a board used to measure the surf.
   - Ⓑ a board that washed up on the beach.
   - Ⓒ a long, narrow board used to ride ocean waves.
   - Ⓓ a board used to keep sharks away.

5. What do Brent and Trey like about Eric? Use examples from the story to tell what they like.

   _____

   _____

6. How does Eric feel at the end of the story? Give examples from the story to support your answer.

   _____

   _____

Name _____ Date _____

Respect All Voices—Wrap-Up

Animal Rights, Animals Wronged

What would life be like without animals? Perhaps you have a pet or wish that you did. Have you ever ridden horseback or visited the zoo? Have you ever watched a squirrel scamper around a tree or watched a bird soar through the air? People use animals in many ways. They are our pets. They entertain us. What, though, do we give back to animals?

> **1. What do you think this passage will be about? Write what you think.**

Uses or Abuses?

Dogs, cats, rabbits, mice, monkeys, and sheep have been used in medical research for many years. Doctors gave these animals diseases, and then the doctors tried to cure them. Because of this research, doctors have been able to prevent cases of diseases like smallpox and rabies. These illnesses were once deadly, but now they are under control. Important research for curing cancer and other diseases continues.

Food and clothing companies depend on animals such as cows, sheep, pigs, chickens, and goats. They are used for their meat, milk, skin, fur, and eggs. Many of these animals spend their entire lives in large factory farms. Factory farms put many animals in very small spaces to save money. The spaces are often cold. Most of them are so small that the animals can't walk or even turn around. Many factories are dark, and animals never see sunlight. Factories don't feel the need to make animals comfortable because they won't be there very long.

Some factory farms raise chickens to lay eggs. Many chickens grow up pressed together in tiny cages. Chickens that don't lay eggs do not get any food or water. Without food or water, chickens become stressed and lay eggs.

> 2. Do people need to use animals in these ways? Tell why you think that.

Out in the Wild

Some people hunt animals for food or sport. They believe that hunting is necessary for the health of animals. During the winter there is less food to be found. Many wild animals slowly starve. Hunting kills off wild animals quickly. The practice of hunting lowers the number of animals looking for food. Therefore, there is more food for the remaining animals, and fewer animals starve to death.

People who don't believe in hunting say that not every animal that gets shot dies right away. Some animals are able to run away, but they are hurt so badly that they die slow, painful deaths.

That's Entertainment?

Animal acts in circuses and rodeos entertain people. Circus animals do tricks for amazed audiences. Would the audience be as pleased if they knew why the animals did those tricks? You might think that a circus animal jumps through fire to get a treat. However, animals are afraid of fire. They jump through fire only when they are more afraid of their trainer than of fire. Trainers use whips, sticks, sharp hooks, and electric shocks to control animals. Circus animals travel to shows in cages. Inside those cages, ropes or chains tie the animals down. Trainers even put ropes over the animals' mouths to keep them from biting.

Rodeos have contests to see who can stay on a horse the longest. The horse kicks terribly while a person tries to hang on. Horses don't always kick naturally. In a rodeo, someone ties a belt very tightly below a horse's stomach. The horse then tries to kick the belt off, but it doesn't work. The person bouncing on the horse hurts the horse's back. Sometimes the pounding of the rider breaks the horse's back.

> **3. Would people enjoy circuses and rodeos if they knew how the animals felt? Write what you think.**

What Does It All Mean?

Many people cannot ignore the cruel treatment that animals suffer. These people support either animal **welfare** or animal rights. People who believe in animal welfare think that humans should be able to use animals for food and clothing. However, these people also believe that animals should not be made to suffer. If animals are going to be used for meat or medicines, they should be treated as gently as possible.

On the other hand, someone who is in favor of animal rights might believe that animals should never be used by people for fur, leather, or meat. People who believe strongly in animal rights often do not eat meat or do not eat certain kinds of meat.

Animals and people will continue living together for many years to come. And people will continue to use animals for a variety of reasons. Can people learn to share this world with other animals in a kind and caring way?

How You Can Help

Here are several things that you can do to make life better for animals.

- **Treat your pets with care.** Feed and water them regularly. Make sure they are warm when the weather is cold. Never leave an animal in a hot, parked car.

- **Volunteer at an animal shelter.** You can make the animals feel safe and happy, and you can help keep their cages clean. Loose dogs and cats are a huge problem. You can also help teach people the importance of reducing the numbers of loose dogs and cats.

- **Change your buying habits.** You might buy fewer clothes or foods that are made from animals. Also, you can buy products that are not tested on animals. Look for labels on the products you buy.

- **Write letters to voice your opinions.** You might write to companies that test their products on animals. You can also write to the people in your community who make laws, telling them about your concern for animals.

- **Provide food for wild animals.** Plant bushes with berries or trees that bear nuts.

- **Find out what you can do to help animals that are close to becoming extinct.** Contact a group that helps wild animals survive.

---

4. What is the most important thing you learned in this passage?

Name _____ Date _____

Respect All Voices—Wrap-Up

 Fill in the circle of the correct answer.

1) This passage is mostly about—
   Ⓐ how to take care of your pet.
   Ⓑ why animals act as they do in rodeos and circuses.
   Ⓒ what animals do to help people.
   Ⓓ how animals are treated badly.

2) Circus and rodeo animals might act the way they do because they—
   Ⓐ were taught to do fun tricks.   Ⓒ are scared or in pain.
   Ⓑ want to get a treat.   Ⓓ like their trainers and riders.

3) What do people who care about animal *welfare* believe?
   Ⓐ People should not eat meat or wear leather.
   Ⓑ People should not make animals suffer.
   Ⓒ People are more important than animals.
   Ⓓ People should not share the world with animals.

4) Why did the author write this passage?
   Ⓐ to convince people to help animals
   Ⓑ to tell interesting stories about animals
   Ⓒ to describe different kinds of animals
   Ⓓ to teach people how to take care of pets

5) What are two ways that you can help animals? Use examples from the passage.

   _____
   _____

6) What does the author of this passage think about animals? Give examples from the passage to support your answer.

   _____
   _____
   _____

Answer Key

Something Rotten at Village Market

page 8
Answers may vary. Sample answers are given.
1. a grocery bagger
2. boring
3. a grocery cashier
4. exciting
5. Customers often tell stories to grocery cashiers.

page 9
1. The first answer is provided.
2. explosion
3. avalanche
4. employee
5. pyramid
6. cashier
7. brawny
8. hesitantly
9. anticipation
10. cash register

pages 10–14
For questions in this section, answers will vary.

page 15
1. B
2. C
3. A
4. D
5. Answers will vary.
6. Answers will vary.

page 16
Answers to the Idea Chart in this section will vary.

page 17
Answers will vary. Check that the topic is clearly defined and supporting details are well developed.

page 18
Answers may vary. Sample answers are given.
Similarities
both work at the store
both teenagers
Differences
Tony: nervous, 14, small
Benny: helpful, 18, big and brawny, the boss

page 19
1. whether
2. guessed
3. raise
4. aloud
Answers may vary. Sample answers are given.
5. The weather is nice outside today.
6. We are having a guest for dinner tonight.
7. The sun's rays can hurt your skin.
8. I am not allowed to have a job.

A Teen's Guide to Working

page 20
For questions in this section, answers will vary.

page 21
1. The first answer is provided.
2. unlimited
3. minimum wage
4. teens
5. benefits
6. trade school
7. mentor
8. guardians
9. socialization skills
10. accumulate

pages 22–26
For questions in this section, answers will vary.

page 27
1. C
2. B
3. A
4. D
5. Answers will vary.
6. Answers will vary.

page 28
Answers to the Planning Chart in this section will vary.

page 29
Answers will vary. Check that the letter fulfills its purpose and is convincing.

page 30
1. Internet
2. Library
3. Job Listings
4. Telephone Book
5. Classified Advertisements

page 31
1. many
2. well
3. earn
4. good
5. know
Answers may vary. Accept all reasonable responses, including:
6. shy
7. perfect
8. quiet
9. loud
10. lawns

Space Play

page 32
For questions in this section, answers will vary.

page 33
Circled letters are noted by ().
1. The first answer is provided.
2. cr(u)cial
3. re(t)rieve
4. grav(i)tational
5. simulatio(n)s
6. (s)alvaged
7. solar (p)anel
8. Virtu(a)l-reality
9. sar(c)astically
10. vid(e)o
Answer: **out in space**

pages 34–38
For questions in this section, answers will vary.

page 39
1. B
2. A
3. D
4. B
5. Answers will vary.
6. Answers will vary.

page 40
Answers for the Idea Chart in this section will vary.

page 41
Answers will vary. Check that the topic is clearly defined and supporting details are well developed.

page 42
Student-drawn pictures will vary.
1. far into the future.
2. a spacecraft traveling from the moon to Venus.
3. Answers to this question will vary depending on the student's picture.

page 43
Answers will vary.

The Moon and Beyond
page 44
For questions in this section, answers will vary.

page 45
1. The first answer has been provided.
2. modules
3. complex
4. mankind
5. significant
6. technology
7. overtake
8. achievement
9. cosmonauts
10. expandable

pages 46–50
For questions in this section, answers will vary.

page 51
1. C
2. B
3. A
4. B
5. Answers will vary.
6. Answers will vary.

page 52
Answers for the Idea Chart will vary.

page 53
Answers will vary. Check that the summary contains no extraneous information.

page 54
Responses will vary.

page 55
1. b
2. c
3. a
Answers may vary.
4. Answer is provided for students.
5. the race was real
6. hard to believe

Take a Stand—Wrap-Up
pages 56–59
For questions in this section, answers will vary.

page 60
1. D
2. A
3. B
4. B
5. Accept all reasonable responses.
6. Accept all reasonable responses.

pages 61–64
For questions in this section, answers will vary.

page 65
1. D
2. B
3. A
4. D
5. Accept all reasonable responses.
6. Accept all reasonable responses.

pages 66–67
For questions in this section, answers will vary.

Why Me?
page 68
For questions in this section, answers will vary.

page 69
1. The first answer is provided.
2. exterminator
3. checkbook
4. facade
5. duplex
6. recliner
7. delved
8. complex
9. emphysema
10. trinket

pages 70–74
For questions in this section, answers will vary.

page 75
1. B
2. C
3. B
4. A
5. Answers will vary.
6. Answers will vary.

page 76
Answers in the Speech Planner will vary.

page 77
Answers will vary. Check that the speech fulfills its purpose and is convincing.

page 78
Answers will vary.

page 79
1. part-time
2. landlady
3. sometime
4. downstairs
5. newsstand
6. something

And Justice for All
page 80
For questions in this section, answers will vary.

page 81
Circled letters are noted by ().
1. The first answer is provided.
2. com(m)itted
3. (p)rosecuting lawyer
4. ju(r)y
5. verd(i)ct
6. (s)aliva
7. c(o)nvict
8. defe(n)dant
9. cli(e)nts
10. accuse(d)
Answer: **imprisoned**

pages 82–86
For questions in this section, answers will vary.

page 87
1. C
2. C
3. D
4. B
5. Answers will vary.
6. Answers will vary.

page 88
Answers for the Idea Chart in this section will vary.

page 89
Answers will vary. Check that the essay is persuasive.

page 90
Passage Title:
The Crime Scene and Evidence
Answers may vary.
1. Kenneth Waters was sent to jail.
2. His sister believed he was innocent.
3. She wanted to help him.
First Section Header:
A Do-It-Yourself Approach
Answers may vary.
4. She decided to go to law school.
5. She learned about evidence.
6. She found out about DNA.
Second Section Header:
What DNA Proved
7. She became a lawyer.
8. She found DNA evidence.
9. Her brother was set free.
Answers may vary.
10. Guilty or Innocent?
11. Working for Justice
12. Free at Last

page 91
1. index
2. volume
3. guide words
4. entry words
Answers may vary. Sample answers are given.
5. breeds of horses
6. horse
7. Horace and hospital
8. equine

Tales from Gull Island
page 92
For questions in this section, answers will vary.

page 93
1. The first answer is provided.
2. blubbered
3. eardrums
4. top-notch
5. waterlogged
6. fathom
7. grimacing
8. jostled
9. feigned
10. splattered

pages 94–98
For questions in this section, answers will vary.

page 99
1. C
2. B
3. C
4. B
5. Answers will vary.
6. Answers will vary.

page 100
Answers for the Idea Chart in this section will vary.

page 101
Answers will vary. Check that the review is convincing.

page 102
Answers will vary. Accept all reasonable responses.

page 103
1. b
2. a
3. a
4. b
5. b
6. a
Answers will vary.

From Zeus to Aliens
page 104
For questions in this section, answers will vary.

page 105
1. The first answer has been provided.
2. humanoid
3. abducted
4. urban
5. weighed
6. compromise
7. mystifying
8. phenomena
9. resided
10. trustworthy

page 106–110
For questions in this section, answers will vary.

page 111
1. C
2. A
3. D
4. A
5. Answers will vary.
6. Answers will vary.

page 112
Answers for the Idea Web in this section will vary.

page 113
Answers will vary. Check that the myth offers an explanation and is interesting and exciting.

page 114
1. 6
2. Old Myths and Modern Monsters
3. Chapter 4: This Really Works!
4. Chapter 5: A Friend of a Friend Told Me
5. Chapter 2: Things That Go Bump in the Night
6. Chapter 3: Are We Alone?
7. 5, 33–38

page 115
1. not
2. again
3. without
4. full of

Respect All Voices—Wrap-Up
pages 116–119
For questions in this section, answers will vary.

page 120
1. A
2. D
3. B
4. C
5. Answers will vary.
6. Answers will vary.

pages 121–124
For questions in this section, answers will vary.

page 125
1. D
2. C
3. B
4. A
5. Answers will vary.
6. Answers will vary.